PREPARING FOR MEDICAL PRACTICE
made ridiculously simple

Daniel M. Lichtstein, M.D.
Associate Professor of Medicine
Department of Medicine
University of Miami School of Medicine
Miami, Florida

MedMaster Inc. Miami

ISBN # 0-940780-38-0

Made in the United Sates of America

Published by
MedMaster, Inc.
P.O. Box 640028
Miami FL 33164

To my wife Shirley, and my children Jason and Micki, for their love, support and inspiration, always.

To my Dad, for his love, and for the example he has set as a husband and a father.

FOREWORD

Daniel M. Lichtstein, M.D. finished his Chief Medical Residency at the University of Miami/Jackson Memorial Hospital Medical Center on June 30, 1978. He was then and continues to be one of the most thoughtful, ethical and talented practitioners of clinical medicine who I have ever had the pleasure of working with. From the day of his departure for private practice in West Palm Beach, Florida until his successful recruitment back to the faculty of the University of Miami on July 1, 1996, I never wavered in my goal to persuade Danny to re-join the academic teaching environment.

He has brought to the training program at the University of Miami a practical and highly ethical view and approach to the private practice of Medicine. In this role he has served as a mentor and advisor to two classes of graduating residents and his seminars on preparing for medical practice have become enormously popular. In this book he shares his experiences, knowledge and wisdom with the entire medical community. I trust you will profit by it; we certainly have.

Laurence B. Gardner, M.D.
Professor and Chairman
Department of Medicine
University of Miami School of Medicine

December 1, 1997

TABLE OF CONTENTS

INTRODUCTION

After completing my training in internal medicine in 1978, I entered private practice in West Palm Beach, Florida and remained in full-time private practice for the next eighteen years. Initially, I was part of a multispecialty group practice, then a small single-specialty group, and finally a large primary care group employed by a hospital organization. In July 1996, I left private practice and joined the faculty of the University of Miami School of Medicine, where I currently serve as the Director of Ambulatory Education for the Department of Medicine.

Traditionally, house staff training programs in internal medicine have concentrated on training interns and residents in general internal medicine or a subspecialty primarily by exposure to inpatient care. Over the past several years, training programs in internal medicine have increased the emphasis on ambulatory medicine, in an attempt to better prepare graduates for careers in private practice. This has, in part, been due to the ever-increasing influence of managed care on physicians' practices, and the reduction of time spent by primary care physicians in the hospital relative to the office.

Despite the increased role of ambulatory training, graduating residents are still poorly prepared to enter private practice. They receive little or no guidance in looking for a job, different job opportunities, reading an employment contract, securing hospital privileges, and negotiating with managed care companies. There is no formal training in how to set up an office, anticipated expenses in doing so, and how to go about finding the right employees. The overall understanding of managed care and it's implications among graduating residents is poor. Training in medical record documentation, dictation, risk management, ethics, and the proper use of consultants is insufficient in most programs. In addition, more emphasis on the patient-physician interaction and relationship would be beneficial to anyone about to enter private practice.

It is the goal of this manual to attempt to better prepare primary care physicians for the world of private practice. Training programs may find that incorporating these guidelines and principles into their goals and objectives will serve to enhance the residents' experiences and allow for a smooth transition from residency to private practice.

CHAPTER 1.

OPPORTUNITIES IN PRIVATE PRACTICE

Up until approximately ten years ago, a graduating resident had only to decide where to practice, and whether to join an established physician or group or open his or her own practice. The changing medical environment has created different and confusing alternatives to traditional private practice. A resident completing training now may open a practice, join an established practice or group, be employed by a hospital-owned entity, work for a managed care company, remain in academic medicine or have other potential employment opportunities from which to choose. Before deciding which avenue to pursue, it is important to understand the similarities and differences among these possibilities.

Traditional private practice still exists in most areas. One can still establish a private practice from scratch, and be successful, in many areas of the country. However, as managed care continues to exert more influence, those geographical areas impacted most by managed care have fewer primary care physicians in traditional private practice and more in employment situations. As a resident begins to consider his options, it is crucial to know how the area he is interested in has been affected by managed care, and whether physicians in traditional private practice are still thriving. The most effective way to do this is to speak with as many physicians in practice as you can, and to ask specific questions about recent changes they have experienced.

Group practices in primary care, subspecialties, and multispecialties exist in most geographical areas. Many groups actively advertise in medical journals for new associates, but it is also a good idea, if interested in a group practice situation, for senior residents to initiate contact themselves, with an introductory letter and copy of one's curriculum vitae. By contacting the medical staff offices of the hospitals in an area, one can obtain names of groups and individual physicians in any specialty.

Over the past several years, hospitals (both for profit and not-for-profit) have increasingly become involved in employing physicians. This opportunity exists both for established physician practices interested in affiliating with the hospital as well as to physicians just completing training interested in an employment situation. Hospital administrators and boards are interested in having primary care physicians who are tied to their institutions, as a way to both capture managed care contracts and to ensure a steady flow of inpatient admissions and ancillary testing.

From the standpoint of the resident who is contemplating such an employment situation, it has both potential advantages and disadvantages. Advantages include a guaranteed salary with possible incentives, no financial investment in setting up the office, and no financial risk in that the employer pays the salaries of the office personnel, as well as other overhead expenses. Malpractice insurance premiums, fees for applying for hospital staff privileges, and license fees are usually paid by the employer. In addition, by affiliating with a hospital, one can usually assume little or no difficulty in becoming a provider for those managed care plans with which you wish to participate. Also, the employer takes responsibility for billing and other business matters of the practice, leaving the physician to practice medicine.

However, there are potential disadvantages as well. Under such an agreement, the physician is an EMPLOYEE. This does limit one's autonomy and independence in the practice setting. The employer may want the physician to participate in managed care plans with which the physician would otherwise not wish to deal. The employed physician may be asked to see more patients on an average day than the physician feels he can comfortably manage while still providing quality care. The employed physician may have no say in the hiring and firing of the other personnel in the office. These, as well as other issues of autonomy, could and should be discussed and agreed upon prior to entering an employment situation.

Physicians considering employment opportunities with a hospital must keep in mind that a hospital may change ownership at any time. This could result in converting a not-for-profit institution to a for-profit one. The hospital's goals and philosophy may change significantly in the process. This may substantially affect an employed physician's standing, and may leave the physician in an uncomfortable practice environment. In this regard, before finalizing an employment contract, consider this possibility, and try to include a clause which would allow you to opt out of a practice situation with which you were not comfortable.

A concept with which any potential employed physician should be thoroughly familiar is the restrictive covenant. This could apply to a physician joining another physician or group or to a physician becoming employed by a hospital or other entity. A restrictive covenant is a clause in a contract which states that if the physician terminates his relationship with the group (or hospital-employer), or the employer or group terminates the relationship with the physician, that the physician cannot practice medicine within a predetermined distance of the former employer for a specified period of time. In other words, if you are employed by a hospital or group, and either decide to leave that situation, not renew after expiration of the original contract, or are asked to leave, you are expected not to practice for several years within the same geographical region. This clause is meant to protect the employer from a physician joining a group, having the group finance the start-up of his practice, help him establish a practice, and then have the physician leave and be a direct competitor. Historically, physicians have challenged this clause, sometimes successfully, but it is still a potential impediment should one wish to leave an undesirable situation.

Managed care organizations are always looking for primary care physicians, both as providers (physicians in private practice who contract with the company to provide services), as well as employed physicians. Physicians employed by managed care companies often are office-based only, in that the company contracts with other physicians to provide hospital services. This may have the advantage of a more controlled, less unpredictable lifestyle, with limited or no night or weekend call. However, for many physicians, it has the disadvantage of not being able to follow your patients in the hospital, and thereby not providing comprehensive care for your patients. There also tends to be pressure on the physician in such circumstances to see a high daily volume of patients.

MAKING THE RIGHT DECISION

Once you have identified a potential job opportunity, and after interviewing with the group, how do you know if it is right for you? There is no way to be absolutely sure, but there are steps you should take to improve the odds. Take several looks at the group. Don't base your decision on one interview or one visit. Arrange to make hospital rounds with the physician(s) with whom you would be working. Speak to other physicians in the area or on the hospital staff about the physician or group with which you are interviewing. Spend time with any physicians who have previously worked with the group, but who are no longer affiliated. They can often provide valuable insight into potential problems for you. Speak extensively with the most recently recruited physicians of the group about their experiences. Always ask for a copy of a contract early in the process for your review, and have an attorney (preferably one dealing with health-care issues) review it. If at all possible, try to avoid restrictive covenants.

Look for opportunities where you are on equal footing with the other physicians. In other words, if you are joining three other primary care physicians, is night and weekend call equally divided? Are you expected to take more emergency room call than the others?

Be sure you fully understand the salary structure. Most employment situations involve a guaranteed base salary, with the potential to make additional income, based on production. However the financial agreement is worded, be sure you fully understand all of its ramifications. If the employment agreement is for a specified length of time (i.e. two years), be sure to understand what happens when that time is up. Is there an automatic renewal clause? Do you become a partner? What does that mean? Is there a "buy-in"—meaning, are you then expected to pay a sum of money to become a partner? If so, of what are you becoming a partner? Does it involve only the professional side of the practice, or does it also involve hard assets, such as office equipment and real estate?

- Take more than one look.
- Obtain as much input as possible about future colleagues.
- Review contract with an attorney.
- Understand the salary structure.

Before getting off of the topic of salary and income, we should define some important terms:

Base Salary: The income, usually yearly, that you are guaranteed to earn, below which your income will not fall.

Threshold: The predetermined dollar amount above which you receive a percentage of collections.

Incentive income: That additional income that you have the potential to earn, but that is not guaranteed. Incentive can be structured in different ways. One of the most common is to earn a predetermined percentage of collections above a set threshold. Example: the threshold is set at $200,000 yearly; you collect $250,000 for the year; it was predetermined in your contract that you would be paid 50% of this difference: i.e., 50% of $50,000 or $25,000.

Collections: That money actually collected for professional services provided by you. This should include prepaid capitation for plans with which you are involved.

Billings: The total dollar amount of bills submitted by you to patients for services provided.

Capitation: This is a term which pertains to your involvement with managed care companies. It is the amount prepaid to you each month for those patients for whom you are responsible under a given managed care plan. For example, you have a contract with Blue Cross HMO to care for 100 patients for $20 per patient (or member) per month. You receive $2,000 monthly in capitation payment from Blue Cross. You receive this whether you see any of the patients that month or not, and, in general, you do not receive any additional money from Blue Cross even if you see each of the patients several times in a given month.

Overhead: That percentage of total collections which is necessary to pay practice expenses, such as rent, employee salaries, supplies, insurance, etc. The overhead percentage varies significantly dependent upon the type of practice it is. Typically, for a primary care practice, it averages 45-55% of total collections.

SOLO VS. GROUP PRACTICE

There are advantages and disadvantages to both solo and group practices. It is important to know your own personality well, and to recognize your strengths and weaknesses before deciding on a specific opportunity. Once again, take the opportunity during your training to speak with physicians in solo practice and in group practice situations about their individual experiences.

The major advantage of solo practice is that you are at all times your own boss. You can establish the practice according to your own preferences, and you avoid conflicts in practice style or practice philosophy. Personality conflicts, common in group practice situations, are avoided. Work ethic may differ significantly among the physicians of a group. Priorities may differ, and the overall goals of physicians in practice together may not be the same. This usually leads to conflicts down the road. In solo practice, you may also recruit an additional physician(s) when you are ready, and have the independence to choose the one(s) with whom you would like to work.

There are disadvantages to the solo practice environment, however. You are either on-call daily, or you must depend on other physicians to cross-cover with you. You may be fortunate to be able to arrange dependable, and high-quality cross-coverage, but it is not always possible to do so. A cross-coverage arrangement may end at any time, even a very inopportune one. In solo practice, you do not normally benefit from the overflow of patients that you would see if joining a busy, established physician(s). You must build your own reputation, and be aggressive in getting out and meeting other physicians. It is important, in this situation, to get the message out to the medical community that you are available to see new patients, do hospital consultations, and often take additional emergency room call to help build your practice.

When in solo practice, you do not benefit from having colleagues at your side every day. In a group practice, you usually have the luxury of having someone in your specialty to discuss a case with, or to help resolve a problem. In my experience, this is a valuable asset of a group practice situation compared to solo practice. In addition, you may be more likely to develop poor practice habits if in solo practice, in that there is no one there to point them out to you.

In general, your standing with managed care companies is less strong when in solo practice compared to a group. There is power in numbers; i.e., a managed care organization is more likely to accept you as a provider if you are joining an established group than if you are starting off on your own. If you do go solo, it is helpful to affiliate in some way with other providers to strengthen your position with the managed care companies with which you are dealing.

It may be easier to expand ancillary services in your office in a group practice compared to solo practice in that you share overhead expenses equally. If you are thinking about adding an expensive piece of equipment, but one that would enhance your practice, you might be more likely to do so if several physicians are sharing in the cost.

When joining a group practice, or signing an employment agreement of any kind, be aware of the clause in your contract discussing the restrictive covenant. This concept has been discussed earlier, but deserves reemphasis. If present in your contract, it stipulates that if you leave the group or employment situation, you agree not to practice for a predetermined period of time within a predetermined distance of the group. In practical terms, you may love the area, you may have developed an excellent practice and reputation, and yet not wish to stay with the group. On the other hand, the group (or other employer) may not wish to offer you partnership or continued employment. In either situation, you have agreed by contract not to stay in the geographical area for several years. If at all possible, try to avoid inclusion of such a clause in your contract. At the very least, be sure you understand it fully before signing.

One other potential disadvantage of group practice is that break-up may be difficult and costly. If you join an established group and eventually become a partner, and at some future point, the group breaks up, this is usually an expensive process, especially if it involves the need to dissolve a common retirement plan. It is generally advisable to maintain separate retirement plans, if possible, even when joining a group practice. This makes separation, if it occurs in the future, much less complicated. Appropriate legal advice on these issues is paramount.

FINANCIAL AND OTHER CONTRACTUAL CONSIDERATIONS

When negotiating with a group, hospital, or managed care organization, no part of the contract is more important to the physician than the one dealing with salary and benefits. Typically, one is offered a base salary, often with potential incentives or bonuses as well. For example, in South Florida, a graduating resident in general internal medicine can expect to be offered a base salary in the range of $105,000-$150,000 annually, with the average being approximately $120,000. This may be guaranteed for one year or at times up to three years, depending upon the details of the contract. Some contracts call for annual increases of about $5,000 for the duration of the agreement. Others allow for an automatic increase in base salary of approximately $5,000 for board certification.

Incentives or bonuses are often built into the initial employment contract. Most incentives are based on productivity. This means that the employed physician may make additional income if his collections exceed a predetermined dollar amount. For example, if your base salary is $120,000, your contract may specify that you will be paid 50% of all collections that exceed $240,000. This number of $240,000 is not strictly arbitrary. It is often based on the percentage overhead for the physicians in the practice. Therefore, if the average overhead is 50%, you need to collect $240,000 before being eligible for incentive pay. Bonuses are sometimes based on performance evaluations. That is, medical record review, quality assurance standards, patient satisfaction surveys, and utilization review may all be used to determine your eligibility for bonuses. This should all be clearly deliniated in the contract, and the evaluations be as objectively based as possible.

It is crucial that your contract is clear with reference to what happens financially upon completion of the contract term. Is the contract renewable, if both sides agree on terms? If it is a group practice, do you become eligible for partnership upon completion of the initial term? If so, what are the financial ramifications of becoming a partner?

Some employment contracts involve a guaranteed salary for the first year, and subsequent to that, the physician's income is based solely on productivity. For example, you may have a base salary of $120,000 the first year, and subsequent to that, you may make 50% of your collections. Be careful with this type of agreement. It is possible, under such an arrangement, that your first-year income may greatly exceed your subsequent annual income, at least for the next several years. If your practice does not grow quickly, if you are seeing a large percentage of managed care patients, or if collections are lagging behind because of an inefficient billing office, or other reason, you may see a significant drop in income. On the other hand, you do have the potential to increase your income if collections are high.

It is important for you to know exactly what counts as "collections" for the services you provide. If the office has a laboratory, are you credited for any of the lab charges? If you do in-office X-ray, are you credited for any part of this? Do you receive credit for the physician interpretation of electrocardiograms? The answer to these questions will make a significant difference in your total collections. Don't leave any of these issues in doubt; you should have clarification of each prior to signing an agreement.

BENEFITS

Most employment contracts have a benefit package that typically includes such things as malpractice insurance, health insurance, disability insurance, vacation, holidays, continuing medical education, professional society memberships, and medical journals.

Malpractice insurance: Traditionally, if you are joining a group practice or being employed by a hospital or managed care organization, the employer will obtain and pay the premiums for your malpractice insurance. The minimum coverage is usually $250,000/$750,000, and costs approximately $10,000 annually. The cost will vary dependent upon the medical specialty, and geographical area. $250,000/$750,000 refers to a maximum coverage of $250,000 per claim, with a maximum aggregate of $750,000 per year (three claims). Many physicians elect to carry more coverage, i.e., $1,000,000/$3,000,000. If you are entering an employment situation, and your employer is going to pay the premium for $250,000/$750,000 coverage, you may contact the insurance company, if you desire, and find out what the difference in premium would be for additional coverage.

Be certain that there is a clause in your contract which stipulates who pays the malpractice insurance premium if your employment is terminated by either side. Under most circumstances, you are responsible for payment of the premium when your employment ends, but there are exceptions to this. It is critical that your malpractice coverage continues, regardless of your employment status.

Health insurance: Health insurance coverage may be provided as a full benefit, or the cost may be deducted from your salary. You may be asked to choose between an HMO, PPO, or fee-for-service plan. Be sure to understand the differences amongst these, as well as the differences in cost, if any. I will define these terms in Chapter 7: Surviving in Managed Care. Health insurance coverage should commence on your first day of employment. Understand what happens to your health insurance coverage if your employment status changes. Are you able to continue coverage by paying the premiums yourself, while attempting to find alternative arrangements?

Disability insurance: It is important to have adequate disability insurance coverage when employment begins. This is usually provided by the employer. You should try to obtain the maximum coverage available. Most insurance companies limit disability to a percentage (60-80%) of your income. The best type of policy to have is one which covers you for your specific occupation. For example, if you are an invasive cardiologist, you would be considered disabled if you were unable to use your hands.

Vacation: The details of vacation benefits vary significantly. You may receive anywhere from two to six weeks of vacation annually. Some contracts require you to complete a full year of employment before being eligible for paid vacation. Some allow you to receive additional income for unused vacation days.

Holidays: Most contracts specify which days are considered paid holidays, so as not to be deducted from vacation time.

Continuing medical education: Some contracts provide for a specific number of days per year for CME, as well as reimbursement for expenses incurred. The reimbursement may range from $1,000 to $2,500 or higher annually.

Professional organizations: Membership dues for professional organizations may be paid by the employer. This may include membership in such organizations as the local Medical Society, the AMA, and the American College of Physicians. Often, the contract may limit to two or three the number of organizations to which the employer will pay dues on your behalf.

Medical journals: There may be a clause stipulating that the employer pays for the annual subscription to several medical journals of your choosing.

Retirement plan: The contract should call for your participation in the employer's retirement plan, the details of which should be clearly stated.

Regardless of the benefit package, it is important that all specifics be stated in the contract. Be sure that the benefits are guaranteed for the life of the contract, and cannot be canceled unilaterally by the employer. Often, you are able to negotiate specifics before finalizing the agreement, and do not hesitate to do so. Remember, once you sign the deal, it is final.

Financial/Contractual Considerations:

- Base Salary
- Incentive clause

- Renewal terms
- Understand definition of "collections"

Benefit Package:

- Malpractice insurance
- Health insurance
- Disability insurance
- Retirement plan
- Vacation/CME

CHAPTER 2.   SETTING UP YOUR PRACTICE

Whether opening a solo practice or beginning an employment contract, there are steps you must take in advance to prepare prior to seeing your first patient. If joining a group or being employed, the group or practice administrator will usually guide you through this process. If going it alone, you must take these steps yourself, and it is never too early to begin the process.

LICENSURE

Whether joining a group practice or starting on your own, licensure in the state in which you are planning to practice is mandatory. Depending on the state, this may be relatively straightforward, or very time-consuming and cumbersome. Complete the application as far in advance of your anticipated start date as possible, and check on the status of the application often. Try to obtain the name of someone in the appropriate state office if possible, and speak to that person each time you call. Licensure costs vary from state to state, but average approximately $350-$500 every two years.

HOSPITAL PRIVILEGES

Obtaining hospital privileges in a timely way is crucial for most physicians entering private practice. Don't assume that obtaining such privileges is automatic. You never give a second thought to being placed on the staff of the hospitals affiliated with your residency, but getting on the staff of community hospitals is a very different situation. Some hospital staffs are "closed," meaning the hospital is not accepting new applications for staff privileges. Others may be "open" for certain specialties, such as pediatrics, but "closed" for others, such as internal medicine. This information may be obtained from the medical staff office of each hospital, the same office you should contact for an application. It should be clear from this discussion that it would be unwise of you to sign a lease for office space or otherwise make other commitments to a geographical area until you are certain you will be able to get on the hospital staff(s) you require. In the same vein, inquire of the staff office if any changes in the near future are anticipated with reference to an "open" or "closed" staff.

When requesting an application for staff privileges, find out how long the process usually takes. Some hospitals require you to be present in the area, with a local office address, before processing or finalizing your application. Often, interviews with members of the hospital's credentials committee are necessary as part of the process. An application fee is normally required, which may range from

$250 to up to $1,000. If you are joining a group or entering an employment situation, this fee is usually paid by your future employer.

Each staff office traditionally has one individual overseeing all applications. It is very helpful to get to know this person, and develop a good working relationship. He, or she, can either stall or hasten the processing of an application in many situations. Whatever you do, do not lose your patience or become demanding in dealing with the staff office. This will only hurt you in the short and long run. If you develop a good working relationship with this office, it can be a source of future referrals for you, as patients often contact the staff office of a hospital to inquire about physicians.

MALPRACTICE

You must have malpractice insurance in effect before staff privileges are finalized, and before seeing patients in the office. It is a good idea to speak with several physicians of your specialty before obtaining a policy. Premiums may differ from one company to another, and other details of the policies may differ as well. Annual costs are usually lower for physicians who do not perform invasive procedures. Malpractice premiums vary from one part of the country to another, and may range from $5,000 annually to significantly higher, depending upon your specialty. The insurance company will usually have various payment plans, so that you do not have to pay the total premium up front.

DEA

You should have a DEA (Drug Enforcement Agency) number in effect prior to beginning practice. Apply for this several months prior to your anticipated start date. This presently costs approximately $210 for two years. To apply, write to the:

United States Department of Justice
Drug Enforcement Administration
Washington, D.C. 20537

When writing, request: Application for Controlled Substance Registration Certificate.

COUNTY AND CITY LICENSES

County and city licenses should be applied for prior to beginning your practice. These costs are approximately $30-$150 annually.

MANAGED CARE PLANS

As early as possible it is wise to find out which managed care organizations in your area are "the big players." If two or three managed care plans dominate the market, it may be critical for you to become a provider with each of them. You can usually obtain such information from other providers in the area. It is not safe for you to assume that all managed care plans are "open," meaning that new applications are being accepted and processed. Some plans have closed provider panels, and this could conceivably shut you off from a significant percentage of the patient population. Contact the provider representative for each plan you are interested in, and request an application. Inquire about whether the plan anticipates closing it's panel at any time soon.

Managed care contracts are not all the same. You must become familiar with the various provisions of the plans, and fully understand the concepts of capitation, withhold, gatekeeping, and incentives. I will discuss these in more detail in the chapter on managed care.

MEDICARE AND MEDICAID

Provider numbers for Medicare and Medicaid are necessary before rendering care to patients covered under these plans. These may be obtained from the respective provider representatives of each plan.

When you contact Medicare, you will be asked whether you wish to be a "participating physician" or "non-participating physician." This is an important distinction, and one which you must understand clearly. A "participating physician" is a provider who has agreed by contract with Medicare to accept "assignment" on all Medicare claims, and bills Medicare directly for same. Medicare pays 80% of the amount approved directly to you, and the patient is responsible for the remaining 20%. For example, you see a patient in the office, and determine the appropriate billing code to be one for which Medicare recognizes a fee of $100. Your office submits the bill to Medicare with an appropriate diagnostic code. Medicare sends you a payment of $80 (Medicare pays 80% of the approved charge). If the patient has supplemental insurance, this policy would then pay the additional $20; if not, the patient is responsible for the payment.

When you are a "participating physician," Medicare includes your name in a booklet which is sent to all Medicare patients in your geographical area. The fee schedule is also slightly higher for "participating physicians" than for "non-participating physicians." Many Medicare patients look for a physician who "participates," so as to limit (or eliminate) their out-of-pocket costs.

A "non-participating physician" bills the patient directly for services provided, but the fees are still subject to a fee schedule determined by Medicare. If you decide not to "participate," you may still accept "assignment" on a case-by-case basis. This means that for an individual patient, you may bill Medicare directly, and bill the patient (or the patient's supplemental insurance) the additional 20%.

It is important to note that you may change your status from "participating physician" to "non-participating physician" or vice-versa on January 1st of each year. Your decision to "participate" or not may be partly based on the percentage of physicians in your specialty in your area who are presently "participating." If the great majority of primary care physicians are "participating," it may be difficult to attract patients if you do not "participate." Medicare can provide you with this information.

If your billing is computerized, you may elect to file all Medicare claims electronically. These "paperless" claims are processed by Medicare more quickly, and usually result in payment to you within 1-2 weeks.

Before leaving the topic of Medicare, it is important to understand the term "assignment." With reference to billing, "assignment" refers to the fact that for an individual encounter with a patient, you agree to bill Medicare (or other insurance carrier) directly for the service rendered, and agree to accept as full payment the Medicare-approved amount. The difference between "assignment" and "participating" is that when you "participate," you have agreed by contract to accept assignment on ALL claims, whereby, when you do not "participate" you may still decide to accept "assignment" on a claim-to-claim basis.

OFFICE SPACE

When joining an established group, or becoming employed by a hospital or managed care organization, you do not ordinarily have to worry about finding office space. However, when starting a solo practice, this becomes a very important concern. You must take into consideration the distance from your home to the office, from your office to the hospital(s), from the populated areas (where your patients will be coming from) to your office, as well as the office itself. If you are a primary care physician, or are in another specialty which requires frequent evening or night trips to the hospital, living within a reasonable distance of the hospital(s) is important. Often, hospital staff bylaws require a physician to be able to physically get to the hospital within a short (15-30 minutes) period of time in able to respond to an emergent or urgent problem.

If you will be on staff at only one hospital, and the hospital has adjacent office space available, it is a good idea to consider this location. The convenience of being able to walk over to the hospital to make rounds, go to the emergency room, review an X-ray, or go to a committee meeting cannot be overemphasized. This location also creates less disruption for your office hours, in that if you must make an unexpected trip to the hospital in the middle of the day, you may not have to cancel or reschedule patients in the process. Financial losses, incurred when patients are canceled or rescheduled, may thus be avoided. Other alternatives include office buildings in which physicians are located whose hospital affiliations are the same as yours will be. The medical staff office of the hospital(s) will provide you with the office addresses of the physicians currently on staff, and may know of some physicians looking to share or sublet office space. Before signing a lease for space, you should be certain that no roadblocks exist with reference to your licensure, hospital privileges, or managed care affiliations. It would be unwise to commit yourself to space only to find out later that the hospital has a "closed" staff, or that you are unable to obtain a state license.

Sharing office space with another physician(s) is sometimes a good way to begin, as well as a method of containing overhead costs. If it is with a physician of the same specialty who has been in practice for a number of years, this may also be a source of patient referrals, as well as an opportunity to cross-cover with someone. With time, more formal affiliations often develop from such initial informal arrangements.

How much space to rent depends on several factors. A primary care physician will usually require two to three examination rooms and one consultation room, in addition to secretarial space, a nursing station, possibly a small laboratory, and adequate space for files. A small kitchen and eating area for the employees is also desirable. If in-office procedures, such as flexible sigmoidoscopy or stress-testing, are part of your practice, additional space is usually necessary. If you anticipate having a second physician join you in the near future, you may wish to consider this when looking for office space at this stage.

Physicians whose daily patient volumes are higher, such as dermatologists, will traditionally require more examination rooms, and those spending the majority of their time in the hospital (surgeons) may require fewer exam rooms and a smaller office. You should tailor the office to your practice, and if possible, take a little more space than you think you might need, as many physicians outgrow their space quickly. It is easier to grow into your space, than to have to move because you have insufficient square footage.

EQUIPMENT

Equipment needs will vary depending upon your specialty. Basic needs for a primary care physician include examination tables, carts or stands for each exam room, examination lamps, blood pressure cuffs (including a thigh-cuff), ophthalmoscope and otoscope for each room, EKG machine, and chairs and exam stools for each room. A centrifuge for laboratory specimens is necessary, as is a small refrigerator for storing certain medications. A microscope is needed if you anticipate doing urine microscopy, wet preps, or reviewing gram stains or peripheral smears.

Your telephone system is critical to the functioning of your practice. It is the access for your patients to reach you, and you should not underestimate it's importance. Asking other physicians about their systems is very helpful, and this gives you comparisons of costs as well. Be certain to have an adequate number of lines, so patients will be able to get through without difficulty. A dedicated line, or lines, for outgoing calls only, is important so that you are able to reach the hospital or a patient without delay. You may also need a line for electronic billing for Medicare claims.

Telephone systems and other office equipment may be purchased outright or leased. Most medical supply companies have lease programs available for any equipment you need, and you may wish to consider this option at the beginning of your practice.

EMPLOYEES

Once again, if joining an established practice or being employed, you do not usually have to find your own employees. In starting solo practice, there is nothing more important than finding the right employee(s). Your employees are an extension of you, and may go a long way towards making your practice successful and thriving, or be a factor in preventing it from being so.

Finding an individual with experience in a private practice setting would be ideal. However, this may be very difficult to accomplish. Personal recommendations from other physicians, or from employees of other physicians, are often helpful. Advertising the position may yield positive results, but in addition to interviewing the candidates, be certain to personally check their references before making a decision. Contacting previous employees of a recently retired or relocated physician may give you the opportunity to hire someone with significant experience.

For a primary care practice that is not procedurally-oriented, and therefore does not require a skilled or trained individual, it is not mandatory to hire a registered nurse as your medical assistant. The most important attributes to look for in an office employee are honesty, reliability, common sense, flexibility, willingness to learn, patience, and the ability to work well with others (patients and fellow employees). Previous experience in a medical office setting is valuable, but do not limit your interview process to such people. If an individual possesses the above-mentioned qualities, he or she can be trained on the job in most practice situations. This applies to both the "front" office position (appointments, insurance, billing, etc.), and the "back" position (direct patient care-related issues). In a solo practice or small group practice, it is extremely helpful to the functioning of the office that all employees learn most or all of the other's responsibilities so as to be capable of covering for one another in the case of illness or absence. When interviewing potential candidates for your office, this should be kept in mind and discussed with each one before making a decision. Hiring a nurse who later refuses to schedule appointments or do other "front office" tasks would be avoidable if these issues are discussed up front.

Office employees who demonstrate respect for your patients and who are well-liked by them assist in the establishment of goodwill, and increase the chances of your practice becoming successful. By the same token, an employee who is rude or disrespectful may be responsible for the loss of patients, regardless of how the patients feel about you. Take your time in making hiring decisions. Finding the right individual(s) may not be easy, but will be well worth it in the long run.

OCCUPATIONAL AND SAFETY HEALTH ADMINISTRATION

All medical offices and physicians must be familiar with and adhere to the regulations as outlined by OSHA (Occupational and Safety Health Administration). Obtain a copy of the regulations directly from OSHA, and read them carefully. Included in these rules are the proper method of disposing of sharp instruments and other medical supplies, the proper handling of laboratory specimens, the requirements for hepatitis B vaccine for employees at risk, and the correct way to handle a needle stick incident.

MEDICAL RECORDS

The charting system you use should be one with which you are comfortable. Many options exist, and you may familiarize yourself with them by contacting the appropriate supply company.

It is important to have a system in place from the start, and to be sure that all employees are familiar with it. How to keep a medical record and other aspects of medical documentation will be thoroughly discussed in an upcoming chapter, but it is imperative that all employees understand and adhere to a basic premise: nothing should be placed in the medical record before you, as the physician of record, have seen it and signed off on it. There should be no exception to this rule.

- Licensure
- Hospital privileges
- Malpractice insurance
- DEA Registration
- County/Occupational Licenses
- Managed Care plans
- Medicare/Medicaid provider numbers
- Office space/Employees

CHAPTER 3.   THE FIRST YEAR

Now that you have set up your practice, and are ready to see patients, where will they come from? Will they come at all? This is a common fear among physicians beginning private practice. There are several steps you can take to attract patients and referrals to your practice.

As mentioned earlier, the sooner you are an active provider for managed care plans, the sooner you will begin to see patients from these plans. The plans will place your name on the list of providers that is sent on a regular basis to both patients and other providers. As soon as you have been accepted as a provider, patients will be able to select you as a primary care physician, or if you are not a primary care physician, they may see you in referral from their primary care physician.

Take the initiative and introduce yourself to as many physicians in your community as you can. When you are making rounds in the hospital, introduce yourself to any physicians you have not yet met. Don't get caught without a handful of business cards at all times. If applicable to your specialty, let it be known clearly that you are willing and interested in seeing patients in consultation, regardless of time of day. Preoperative consultations are an excellent source of patients (and income) for a physician starting out, and a good way for surgeons to get to know you. Let the surgeons in town know that you are available to perform these evaluations. These same surgeons will probably then become a valuable source of referrals to your office as well.

Many community hospitals require their physicians to take emergency room call. This is especially true of a community hospital without an affiliated house staff training program. Emergency room call means that for a given shift (usually 24 hours), you are on-call for your specialty to be responsible to evaluate and admit patients who present without a physician. For example, a patient presents to the emergency room in acute pulmonary edema, and does not have a physician. The patient is seen and evaluated by the emergency room physician, who will usually then initiate treatment. You, as the internist on-call, would be contacted, and it would then be your responsibility to admit and care for the patient during the hospital stay.

The frequency with which you take emergency room call varies depending on the number of physicians on staff who are sharing these duties. Some hospitals excuse physicians from this responsibility after serving for a certain number of years, i.e. 10-15 years. Taking additional emergency room call when you first start practice is often an effective way to help build your practice. Physicians who have been in practice for several years, and who are busy in the office, are frequently happy to give up their call to a new physician in town. For the physician starting out, it is a way to be more visible in the hospital, have a larger census of inpatients, increase billings, work with subspecialists and surgeons, and overall be busier than you otherwise would be at this stage. It also sends an important message to the medical community about yourself, which is that you are anxious and willing to work hard and do what it takes to have a successful practice.

Some hospitals pay a flat rate to physicians per emergency room on-call shift. This is a good source of income for the physician in the early years of practice, until the office practice becomes busier. It is important to realize that being on-call for the emergency room does not mean that you are the ER physician. The ER physician is full-time in the ER, and contacts you if a patient requires admission or if he wishes you to see a patient in consultation.

Introduce yourself to all the nursing and other ancillary personnel of the hospital. These individuals assist you greatly in the care of your patients, and may also become patients of yours or refer patients to you.

If your hospital(s) has a speaker's program whereby staff members give talks about health-related matters, become involved in this. Get out into the community and speak to groups, including, but not limited to, retirees, civic groups, and schools. Often the managed care organizations with which you are working can arrange for you to address groups of patients, and if so, be sure to bring along your business cards.

In the early stages of your practice, consider having additional office hours when most other physicians of your specialty do not. Being available, and advertising these hours, may attract patients who, for various reasons, are unable to see a physician during regular hours. Keeping the office open one evening each week until 7 or 8 o'clock and/or having office hours Saturday morning should be considered.

If beginning solo practice, or otherwise being in a situation whereby your income is strictly dependent upon your collections, it is tempting for a physician to try to maximize billings or charges for an individual patient. Try to avoid this trap. If it appears to a patient or to a referring physician that you are overcharging or doing unnecessary tests, you are likely to lose the patient or the referral source. Remain at all times both intellectually and financially honest. By doing so, you will establish a good reputation among your patients and your peers, and business will flourish with time. If your reputation at the outset is anything but ethical and honest, you may never be able to overcome this.

During the early stages of private practice, a significant percentage of your patients come from referrals from other physicians or other health care personnel, as well as from the managed care plans with which you are working. However, with time, many of the patients you see, particularly those paying fee-for-service, are referred by other patients you have seen. If you are perceived by your patients as caring and concerned, and you are available to them when they need you, your best referral base will be your own patients. This is especially true for primary care practices, but applies to all other physicians as well.

There are several things you can do in the care of your patients that might set you apart from other providers. The suggestions which follow are not meant to be all-inclusive, but are a good framework from which to start. Try to see your patients as close to their scheduled appointment times as possible. This is extremely important to most patients, and is one of the most frequent complaints voiced about physicians by patients. The first mistake physicians make relative to this is to start late; if you are late for your first patient of the day, you likely will never catch up. If you are running late, be sure that one of your employees informs the patients of this, and how long the wait is anticipated to be. When you do enter the exam room, apologize to the patient for being late, and if it was because of an emergency, inform the patient of that fact.

After you have completed the examination, be certain to explain your findings and recommendations to the patient, and allow sufficient time for questions. If any other family members have accompanied the patient to the office, bring them back to your office to meet you, and give them the chance to ask questions as well. Remember, these family members are also potential patients.

In the early stages of your practice, it is a good idea to personally call patients in order to discuss results of any tests which had been done. This affords the patient the opportunity to ask any questions not asked at the office visit, and demonstrates your concern and interest in the patient. Patients often have significant anxiety about the results of tests, and appreciate hearing from you as soon as possible after the tests have been completed. Try to put yourself in the place of the patient, and treat the patient the way you would want to be treated. If you will be out of your office for a period of time on vacation or at a meeting, try to avoid scheduling radiologic procedures, such as mammograms, during that time. It is not reasonable to expect a patient, already anxious about the results, to have to wait 1-2 weeks to hear form you. This type of consideration is definitely appreciated by most patients.

Unsolicited telephone calls to a patient to see how he or she is doing create excellent rapport. If you have recently discharged someone from the hospital, calling the patient the next day to check on his condition is good medicine and demonstrates your concern as well. It gives you the opportunity to review the patient's medications, be sure a follow-up appointment has been made, answer any questions, and obtain a progress report from the patient. A similar phone call to an ill patient you had seen in the office the previous day to check on his or her progress is advisable. These simple acts, which are not very time-consuming, can go a long way in creating strong relationships with your patients, and also help in building your practice.

Availability and accessibility are critical components to a successful practice. Making time the same day to evaluate a new patient being referred by another patient or by a physician will pay off for you in the long run. On the other hand, if you say no, especially to a referring physician, you may not see additional patients from that doctor in the future. By the same token, being accessible to your established patients is extremely important. If your own patients cannot speak to you or schedule appointments in a timely way, you will more than likely lose them. Establish a routine in the office for returning phone calls from patients. Be certain that your office personnel bring to your attention immediately any message which indicates an urgent or emergent problem. If the call is not urgent, your employees should inform the patient when to expect a call back. Many physicians return these calls during the lunch hour, or at the end of the day. However, you may find that you are able to return some calls between patient visits, especially if you are not running behind schedule.

Early in your practice career you usually have extra time to spend with patients. Take full advantage of this. An additional five or ten minutes with someone may leave a lasting impression, and will be time well spent and invested. If you look back at your practice after a number of years, you will realize that a significant percentage of your patients were either directly or indirectly referred from some of the individuals you cared for in the first few years.

- Managed Care Plans
- Take the initiative
- Emergency room call
- Speaker's programs
- AVAILABILITY
- ACCESSIBILITY

CHAPTER 4.

MEDICAL RECORD DOCUMENTATION

During residency, physicians receive little formal training in proper medical record documentation. This applies to both the inpatient and outpatient arenas. A well-documented medical record serves several important functions. It is the history of the patient's care, and therefore serves as your reference for each person. Quality of care is improved in that a well-organized and complete record allows you to accurately track such things as allergies, medications, refills, preventive care, immunizations, and current or active medical problems. A thorough and legible record may be your best defense in a malpractice claim. I have heard attorneys say, "If you didn't write it down, you didn't do it," meaning that written documentation is your best proof of treatment or recommendations provided to a patient. All notes should be dated and signed.

If you hand write your office notes, be sure they are clearly legible. The same thing applies to notes in the hospital chart. If your handwriting is beyond repair, it would be advisable to dictate your notes. This service may be available in the hospital as well. If you do dictate, be sure to carefully read the dictation before signing, because by signing you are attesting to the accuracy of the report.

You can never be too thorough in record documentation. Anything and everything which applies to the medical care of a patient should be documented in the chart. You should have a note for each office visit. All medication refills should be documented, including the number of pills for each prescription. All phone calls dealing with symptoms, advice, recommendations, or test results should be charted. If a patient fails to keep an appointment to see you or does not appear for an X-ray or other diagnostic test, be sure to write it in the chart. It is advisable to ask your office to contact any patient who has not appeared for an appointment to find out the reason, if possible, and to reschedule, if necessary. By making this contact with the patient and charting it, you have also documented your recommendations again.

Proper documentation is critical in the circumstance when a patient does not follow your instructions or advice. If you recommend hospitalization, and the patient refuses, document that clearly in the record. If a patient refuses to undergo a test or procedure which you feel is medically necessary, state that in your note. If compliance with medications or diet is a problem, it is important that this is reflected in the medical record.

When prescribing new medication for someone, it is proper to discuss potential adverse effects. You should include mention of these discussions in the record, and also state what you have instructed the patient to do in the event of such adverse reactions. Remember the potential for drug-drug interactions, and be sure you are aware of all other medications the patient is presently taking. Be sure your record is up to date with reference to each patient's allergies.

If an office visit is generated by a symptom or illness, at the end of your note it is appropriate to document that you have instructed the patient to contact you if the symptoms persist or change in any way, or should any new problem occur. Even though you may have verbalized this to the patient, if you do not document it, you may leave yourself liable should a complication occur. WRITE IT DOWN!!

At the completion of each entry in the record, you should clearly state what the plan of treatment and follow-up is. If medication is being prescribed, be certain to state the duration of treatment. If you have asked the patient to schedule a return appointment, state that fact in the record. If the office visit generates a referral to another physician, state clearly that you are making the referral, the reason for doing so, and whether the patient or your office is making the appointment.

Develop a method for tracking of laboratory results, radiologic studies, and other diagnostic tests you have performed or scheduled for your patients. Some offices tell their patients, "if you don't hear from us, it means everything was fine." There is significant risk in this system, in that if you, as the ordering physician, do not receive the result, and it is abnormal, you may become aware of it too late. If you record each laboratory test performed and sent to a reference lab, your nurse can cross-check the record when the results are received. By keeping a log of radiologic studies ordered, by date the test is to be performed, you will know whether you have received the report or whether the patient may have failed to keep the appointment. You should request that you be contacted by phone directly by the lab or radiologist of any clinically significant abnormality. Anything less than that is taking a chance that you may not receive an important result in a timely way. If the lab or diagnostic center fails to work closely with you on this point, you should find alternative ancillary centers.

Many physicians find it helpful to have a separate page in the front of each chart to accurately keep track of, and refer to, a record of medications, allergies, immunizations, preventive health measures (mammograms, colon cancer screening, etc.), active problems, and other details for the individual patient. You can design this page to fit your practice and style.

Often, after reading your dictation or your handwritten note, you realize you have made a mistake and wish to correct it. Never "white-out" an entry in the record, and do not cross something out so extensively that it cannot be read. The proper way to make a correction is to draw a single straight line through the entry, write the correction, initial it and date it. By doing this, the incorrect entry should still be readable. If you wish to make an addition or addendum, label the entry accordingly (addition or addendum), write the entry, initial it and date it.

Always use the correct date when making an entry in the chart. If you spoke to a patient by phone at night, when you write the note the next day, start with that day's date, and make the proper entry. For example:

June 9, 1997: Telephone call with Mrs. Smith 6/8/97, 11pm: The patient called with abdominal pain, temperature of 101, and nausea. I advised her to go to the emergency room for evaluation. She agreed to do so. DML.

As a general rule, you should read all entries made in the chart by your office personnel. Make it clear to everyone in your office that you should be given the chart for review of any patient about whom an entry in the record has occurred. Medication refills, as mentioned previously, should always be charted. If the refill request is for a controlled drug, such as a narcotic analgesic, tranquilizer, or sleeping pill, you should approve it prior to your office personnel contacting the pharmacy. It is wise to make this a standing policy in your office.

Thorough and clear documentation is crucial if a patient is not going to follow your recommendations. If the patient is acutely ill, and you have recommended hospitalization, if the patient refuses, you should document not only that hospitalization has been refused, but that you have warned the patient (preferably in the presence of family members as well) of potential consequences, including possible death. It may be appropriate to ask the patient to sign an AMA ("against medical advice") form, but proper documentation in the chart is still mandatory.

All physicians should be thoroughly familiar with the issue of "informed consent." This applies not only to surgical procedures, but to any therapeutic or diagnostic test which may place the patient at risk. "Informed consent" means that you have informed the patient, in a way that is comprehensible to him, of potential risks and benefits of the procedure or treatment which you are recommending, and alternatives to such so that the patient may decide whether to proceed. If the procedure is an invasive one, an informed consent form, properly executed by the patient, is appropriate. However, for most treatment options outlined by a primary care physician, informed consent does not involve a separate form, but should be documented in the medical record nonetheless.

It is good practice to document when you have called to discuss results of tests with a patient. If you have recommended a repeat laboratory study, document that you have informed the patient of this, and when it is to be. Always notate such a phone call, even if the results were normal.

In today's society, physicians like virtually everyone else, find themselves speaking to answering machines as often as to people. If leaving a message on a machine, be certain to document in the chart that you have done so, and make it clear as to who (the patient or you) is responsible to return the call. Never leave specific details of test results on a message machine so as not to risk compromising patient confidentiality.

- Write legibly
- Sign and date all notes
- Be thorough
- Flow sheet/Problem list
- CONFIDENTIALITY

CHAPTER 5.

RISK MANAGEMENT AND MALPRACTICE PREVENTION

No health care provider is immune from the threat of medical malpractice. It is out there and not about to disappear anytime soon. Unfortunately, the threat of potential malpractice has lead to a huge increase in health care expenditures, not in small part due to physicians' fears of "missing something." How should a physician starting out in practice deal with this? There is no simple answer, but understanding the playing field is a good start.

Most adverse events do not result in malpractice claims. The establishment of a strong patient-physician relationship based on honesty, trust, and communication is one of the best methods of prevention. This cannot be overemphasized. If your patients see you as someone who cares about them and has their best interests in mind, they are less likely to involve you in a malpractice claim. Be open and honest with your patients about their health status, and about results of all exams and tests. Avoid guarantees or promises about outcomes of treatment at all times.

Try to keep patient expectations realistic, and never be afraid to say, "I don't know." None of us have all of the answers, and no one should expect us to. Physicians who often find themselves in court are ones who did not ask for help when it would have been appropriate to do so, or ones who perform procedures which they were not specifically trained to do. Learn to use consultants properly and appropriately, and never be afraid to call one to assist you with a difficult or confusing case. Understand the concept of "standard of care." This refers to the standard to which you, as a physician, are held, when the care you have provided is being evaluated. The standard is defined as the care a patient can reasonably be expected to receive from a physician of similar training and experience in your geographical area. For example, if you are in general practice in a rural community without subspecialty support, and are caring for a patient with an acute myocardial infarction, you will be held to a different standard of care than if you practicing in an urban setting with cardiologists on every corner.

It is a sign of strength, rather than weakness, to admit that you may need assistance in the care of a given patient. Your patients will respect your honesty in such matters, and almost always accept your recommendation to consult another physician if you have explained that you feel it is in their best interests to do so. It is not uncommon for a patient to initiate the discussion about a consultant. If a patient wishes you to call a specialist, it is usually a wise idea to proceed. If you talk a patient out of it, and do not call the consultant, if the patient subsequently has a complication, you may find yourself in litigation. This does not imply that, if you feel the patient's request is completely inappropriate, you should not discuss it further.

Whatever the outcome of the discussion, the patient should agree with the decision, and you should document such in the patient's medical record.

Physicians frequently find themselves in a situation where they may feel the care and treatment rendered to a patient by another physician was below the standard of care. Under such circumstances, avoid criticism of the other health care professional in front of the patient. Such open criticism may lead to the initiation of a malpractice claim.

As discussed in the section on medical record documentation, correct and thorough documentation is critical to either avoidance of a malpractice claim or defense of one. Your chart is your defense. If it isn't in the chart, it is assumed it did not occur. This applies to discussions about risks of treatment and procedures, as well as to recommendations for preventive health measures. If you have advised a patient to follow a diet in an attempt to reduce his cholesterol, document it in the record. If you have consulted another physician about a particular patient, be sure to carefully read the consultant's recommendations. This applies to both inpatient and outpatient care. If you do not plan to follow the consultant's recommendations, document in the record the reason(s) why, and also discuss it with the patient. In the circumstance when you are the consultant, it is proper both to call the referring physician with your findings and recommendations, and to dictate or write a formal consultation as well. The proper use of consultants will be discussed further in a subsequent section.

Understand and recognize your own limitations. If you have been trained in a procedure, perform it on a regular basis, do it well, and it falls under your malpractice coverage, it is appropriate for it to be part of your practice. When applying for hospital staff privileges, you will usually be asked to complete a "privilege request form." This is a form on which you will list those procedures for which you wish formal privileges to perform in the hospital. These include such things as thoracentesis, Swan-Ganz catheterization, endotracheal intubation, lumbar puncture, and ventilator management. If a procedure has been part of your residency training, and you want to be able to perform it in the hospital, you should include it on the request form. The credentials committee of the hospital may ask for documentation from your residency program director before approving your request. You place yourself at risk from a malpractice standpoint if you perform a procedure electively for which you do not have privileges.

Office procedures are somewhat different, in that no formal request for privileges is indicated. However, you need to be sure that your malpractice carrier has agreed to cover you for any procedure you may perform in the office. If you are a primary care physician, you are generally looked at by the insurance company as a "non-procedure oriented" physician, and in that view, your premiums for coverage are lower than physicians performing invasive procedures. Therefore, if you fall into the category of a "non-procedure oriented" physician, and you plan on adding a procedure to your office practice (such as stress testing or flexible sigmoidoscopy), be sure to contact your malpractice carrier first.

The standard of care for physicians of your specialty in your area is important to know. If you practice in an area where there is an abundancy of subspecialists in all medical disciplines, and the standard of care is for cardiologists to perform and interpret echocardiograms, it may not be appropriate for you to venture into this area of testing. If you do, and if you subsequently make an error, it could be determined that you were practicing below the "standard of care." Always keep this in mind when deciding whether to perform a procedure yourself or to call a consultant.

Managed care has added another dimension to the malpractice equation. There is often pressure on physicians to shorten hospital length of stays, avoid expensive diagnostic procedures, or limit the use of consultants when caring for patients under a managed care plan. Let's address the question of hospital stays first. Most physicians in private practice have heard a patient or family member of a patient claim that the "hospital" discharged him prematurely, which then led to a complication. Remember, only a physician can discharge a patient from the hospital. Utilization committees, representing the hospital or a managed care plan, may apply pressure on a physician to discharge a patient, but the ultimate order must be written by the physician, and the ultimate responsibility lies on the physician's shoulders. Write the discharge order only when you are comfortable that the patient is stable and ready for discharge, and base this decision on the medical status of the patient. It is appropriate and often necessary to solicit assistance from social service or other personnel in arranging for home care, nursing home transfer or other disposition, and the earlier this is started during hospitalization, the better.

The pressure from managed care to limit costs applies also to the use of diagnostic procedures. Physicians every day find themselves considering which test or medication to order, and in the case of caring for patients in managed care plans, frequently make decisions based on expense. This is a very difficult area for many. Drug formularies may exist which do not include medication that you feel may be best for a given clinical situation. A managed care plan may not approve an expensive test (MRI), despite your feeling that it is medically necessary. The contract you signed with a given plan may call for a bonus for you for keeping expenditures below a certain level. In treating any condition, if two medications are equally effective and well-tolerated, prescribe the less expensive one. However, if it is your judgment that a more expensive medication (or one not on the managed care company's formulary), is superior, inform your patient of this and involve the patient in the decision-making process. It is appropriate in this circumstance to let the patient know which treatment you feel is best, and that to receive it may entail out-of-pocket expense. The patient will then make the final decision. If you base your recommendation solely on financial considerations, you are doing a disservice to your patient.

Similarly, managed care companies may include financial incentives for you to limit your use of consultants. You may be eligible for bonus payments at the end of the year if there is money remaining in the "specialty fund" for the patients under your care. Do not allow this to affect the way you care for patients. If you feel it is medically necessary for a patient to see a specialist, you should proceed with the referral. Do not let potential financial gain change the way you practice. You are leaving yourself vulnerable to malpractice claims if a referral is not generated because of such concerns. Always be an advocate for your patients, and do what you feel is in their best interests at all times.

Ongoing in-service education of your office personnel is an important ingredient in malpractice prevention. Your employees are an extension of you, and you are responsible for their actions. Review on a regular basis your office policies with reference to phone calls, charting, review of laboratory and radiologic results, and all other aspects of patient care. As noted earlier, you should see all reports before being filed in the chart. You should be aware of all telephone calls involving symptomatic patients, even if your nurse or medical assistant initially speaks with the patient. Be certain that your office personnel are well-versed in how to prioritize phone calls, so there is no delay in dealing with urgent problems. These are all important measures in reducing your malpractice risk. Appropriate follow-up of abnormal findings is crucial in malpractice prevention, as is dealing thoroughly with unclear symptoms. For example, the discovery of iron-deficiency in a 60 year-old man should lead to evaluation for possible gastrointestinal malignancy. A palpable breast nodule may require surgical evaluation, despite a normal mammogram. A patient who presents with loss of appetite and weight loss should be thoroughly evaluated to exclude an underlying malignancy, metabolic disorder, or depression. If you have evaluated a patient with new onset of symptoms, and the diagnosis is not clear, be certain to arrange for appropriate timely follow-up and instruct the patient on how to proceed should the situation worsen or change. This latter circumstance is an example of when an unsolicited phone call to the patient is both good medicine and a way to demonstrate your concern.

Most physicians are instructed by their malpractice insurance company as to how to proceed if an intent-to-sue letter is received or a suit filed. It is extremely important that you make no changes of any kind to the medical record at this time. This underlines the point earlier that changes or corrections in the medical record made previously be done correctly, initialed and dated, so it is clear as to who made the entry, and when it was made.

- Establish strong patient-physician relationships
- Avoid making guarantees
- Keep patient's expectations realistic
- Use consultants properly
- Thorough documentation
- Understand "standard of care"
- BE AN ADVOCATE FOR YOUR PATIENT
- In-office risk management

CHAPTER 6.   USE OF CONSULTANTS

During training, despite the frequent use of consultants by residents, there is little or no formal training in this aspect of medicine. Housestaff call consultants when in need of a special procedure, at the request of their attending, for diagnostic assistance, or for treatment alternatives. It is not very different than this in private practice, however, general guidelines for the proper use of consultants will be discussed.

When you feel it is medically indicated to call a consultant, discuss it first with the patient. Explain to the patient, in terms which the patient can understand, the reason for the consultation. Ask the patient if he or she has seen a specialist in that field before, and if so, the patient may request that you contact that physician. In the managed care environment, it is important at this stage to determine which physicians of the specialty in question are "on the plan." The patient may request that you call someone who is not on their plan, and if so, the patient must understand the possible financial ramifications of this. If the patient leaves the decision up to you, as is usually the case, it is then appropriate to contact the consultant you feel is most qualified to address the problem. If you then determine that a particular physician will be seeing your patient, inform the patient of the consultant's name, and in an inpatient situation, when the consultant will be coming. Explain to the patient that you are not removing yourself from the case, and that you will discuss the consultant's findings in detail.

When contacting the consultant, do so yourself, by phone. Do not simply write an order in the chart to "consult Dr. Jones, general surgery." Do not leave it up to the ward secretary in the hospital to call the consultant. It is common courtesy and good medicine to place the call yourself for several reasons. By speaking directly with the physician, you know for certain that he or she has received the request, and that the physician will be able to see your patient. If you feel the situation warrants an urgent consultation, you should communicate this yourself. It affords you the opportunity to provide the consultant with specific clinical information about the patient, and to detail exactly what you wish the consultant to address. If you feel the patient requires a procedure, let the consultant know at this point that that is what you are thinking. You may also ask at this point that the consultant call you after seeing the patient to discuss the pertinent findings and recommendations. If you feel it is appropriate and wish the consultant to follow the patient with you in the hospital, make this clear during your initial conversation.

A consultant's recommendations are just that, recommendations. If you wish the consultant to write orders on your patient, let him know that it is acceptable to you. However, if recommendations are made with which you do not agree, you are by no means obligated to carry them out. You should proceed with a course of action that you feel is in the best interests of your patient. If you decide not to follow a consultant's recommendations, document the reason in the medical record, and discuss it with the patient.

When acting as a consultant, your role is quite different. Thank the referring physician for calling you, and try to see the patient in a timely way. If the referring physician does not specify exactly what he wishes you to address, it is appropriate to ask the question yourself. Is the consult for a procedure only, or does the request include following the patient subsequent to the procedure? Does the referring physician want you to write orders? Let the referring physician know that you will contact him after you have seen the patient to discuss the case. Inquire of the referring physician whether the patient has been informed of the upcoming consultation.

Introduce yourself to the patient at the outset, and be sure the patient knows you are involved at the request of his or her physician. Let the patient know what problem you have been asked to address. Explain your role, and if a procedure is anticipated, explain the details of it, and give the patient the opportunity to ask questions. Make it clear that you will be discussing your findings and recommendations with the referring physician as soon as you have completed your evaluation.

Documentation of the consultation is necessary and important. Begin your note with a statement that you have been asked to see the patient in consultation by Dr. Smith. I suggest writing your findings and recommendations next, so as to make it easier for the referring physician to immediately focus on these points. Many consultants document a complete history and physical exam in the note, but most of these facts have already been obtained by the primary physician. New, pertinent information uncovered should become part of the record, and should be discussed with the referring physician. It is important to write as part of your consultation that you have discussed your findings and recommendations with the referring physician, and it should be clear from the record whether you will be following the patient subsequent to the first visit. Ending your note with a statement, "Thank you for the consultation. I will follow the patient closely with you," is appropriate and clear.

During residency training, it is not uncommon for a consultant to make uncomplimentary remarks about the referring physician, at times, in front of nursing personnel or the patient. The consultant may feel that the request was inappropriate, and that the referring physician should have been able to take care of the problem or perform the procedure. Whatever the reason, it is unprofessional and unethical to make such remarks. In private practice, any suggestion or implication that the referring physician was incompetent or that the consultation was unnecessary, is a certain way to be sure you will never see another patient in referral from that individual. In addition, you may place doubt in the patient's mind about his or her physician or about you. Refrain from expressing such comments under any circumstances.

In the outpatient setting, in addition to providing prompt consultation and immediate feedback to the referring physician, a letter outlining your findings and recommendations is appropriate. This is important for the referring physician's chart; some physicians dictate a cover letter expressing appreciation for the referral, and enclose a copy of the dictated office note for the details. Either one is acceptable. Timeliness is very important, as well.

Under some circumstances, after you have seen a patient in consultation, the patient may ask you to assume primary care. This is a very sensitive area. You may be a medical subspecialist (cardiologist) who also provides primary care. In general, your response should be that you were asked to see the patient in consultation only, and that the patient should return to the original referring physician. Make the referring physician aware of the patient's request, since he or she may not have known about the patient's level of dissatisfaction. If you agree to assume primary care at this point, you risk alienating the referring physician, and losing a referral source for the future. If at a future date, the patient returns to you and states that he or she is no longer seeing the original physician, it is ethical to assume care, but a good idea to inform the patient's original physician of what has transpired. If it can be interpreted at all in the eyes of the referring physician that you had actively attempted to "steal the patient," you will hurt yourself significantly in the long run.

As mentioned above, each managed care plan with which you participate probably has a different list of providers for virtually every specialty. When arranging a consultation, you must be aware of this list, so as not to place the patient at additional financial risk. Situations will undoubtedly arise when you feel that a specialist outside of the plan is more qualified or better suited for a specific problem or particular patient. Handle such a situation with great care. It would not be unethical or inappropriate to inform a patient that the individual you feel would be the best, under the circumstances, is not a provider for the patient's plan. However, avoid making negative statements about the physicians who are participants. If you do not know anything about the physicians listed, let the patient know this. The patient will make the ultimate decision as to whether to see someone on the plan or outside the plan, but be sure the patient is aware of the potential costs of the latter.

- Communicate with your patient
- Contact consultants yourself
- Discuss findings and recommendations with consultant
- Document in the medical record

CHAPTER 7.   SURVIVING IN MANAGED CARE

The explosive growth in health care expenditures has led to what is referred to as managed care. Managed care may be defined as the system of health care delivery which attempts to manage the costs of health care, as well as the access to and quality of that care. It is important for the practicing physician to understand the definition of the following terms:

HEALTH MAINTENANCE ORGANIZATION (HMO): An HMO is an organization which provides comprehensive health care services to an enrolled population for a predetermined sum of money, paid in advance, for a specific length of time. Primary care physicians who become providers for an HMO will traditionally receive payment from the HMO monthly, in advance, for the provision of care to patients who have chosen or been assigned to the physician. The patients are usually responsible for a co-payment (e.g., $10) for each encounter with the physician.

STAFF-MODEL HMO: This is an HMO in which physicians are salaried employees of the HMO, and see only patients enrolled in that particular HMO. Medical care is provided in an office owned by the HMO.

PREFERRED PROVIDER ORGANIZATION (PPO): A PPO is an organization which contracts with an employer to provide health care services to their employees. The PPO receives the health care dollars from the employer, and contracts with physicians and hospitals to provide care. The patient members of the PPO may see any physician on this preferred-provider list. Both the participating physicians and hospitals have agreed in advance to bill the PPO at discounted rates. From a primary care physician's point of view, if an employer (such as the county school board) controls the health care for a large number of patients in a given geographical region, it would be important to be a participating provider for a PPO which has contracted with that employer.

FEE-FOR-SERVICE: This refers to payment for services at the time the service is provided. The patient is billed for each service provided at the time of the visit, and is responsible for the bill. The patient then files a claim with his or her insurance company for reimbursement.

INDEPENDENT PRACTICE ASSOCIATION: This is a network of physicians, practicing in their own offices, which contracts with managed care organizations to provide care to enrollees of the managed care plans. The network negotiates payment rates with the plans as a single entity, representing all of the physicians of the IPA. In this model, the physicians may receive payment both through fee-for-service (usually discounted) or through capitation.

Competency, caring, and availability on the part of a practicing physician used to guarantee that patients would come, but we must now add to the list, being a provider for the managed care plan to which the patients belong. Patients from all groups, including Medicare, Medicaid, and employed fall into this category. To be successful today, all physicians must understand managed care and the effect it may have on your practice.

Start by learning what the penetration of managed care in your geographical area is, and whether it is increasing, and if so, by how much. Practicing physicians in the area as well as the hospitals can usually tell you what percentage of patients are covered by managed care plans. In some markets, 50% or more of the patients are in such plans, and in other areas, it may be as low as 10-15%. If the penetration is significant, it may be critical for you to become a provider for the "big players" in order to be successful. If the largest employer in your area works with a plan which has a closed panel (meaning you cannot become a provider), you may have a very difficult time attracting patients.

Find out which plans in the area cover the most "lives," and whether the provider panels are open. At times, a panel may be closed to an individual physician starting solo practice, but may be open to a physician joining or affiliating with a physician already on the list. There is power in numbers, in that a physician in solo practice tends to have very little influence on managed care organizations, whereby physicians aligned with each other (such as in an IPA) may more easily become providers, and may have more say in matters such as fee schedules and approval of referrals. A physician starting out would be wise to contact existing IPAs, speak to their members, and consider the ramifications of participating.

Knowing the managed care plans with which your prospective hospital(s) works is important in that you may be better able to be accepted as a provider if the managed care organization has an agreement already in place with the hospital(s).

Physicians should be aware that a managed care plan may operate as a "closed panel model." This means that the plan contracts with physicians on an exclusive basis, and that by signing an agreement with such a plan, the physician is agreeing not to contract with other managed care organizations.

How do you know if a given managed care plan's guidelines will allow you to practice quality, cost-effective medicine? Try to learn as much about a plan as you can before signing an agreement. Speak to physicians who have been working with the plan. Request that the plan administrator provide you with a current list of the providers, as well as the names of the physicians who did not renew their contracts with the plan, so you may speak with them as well. Meet with the plan administrator and medical director to learn what methods the plan utilizes for authorization of diagnostic testing and referrals. Is approval very time-consuming? Inquire as to what the appeals process of an adverse decision is. If you feel a patient requires an MRI scan, and it is not approved, what steps can you take? Find out how often the plan does not authorize diagnostic testing or referrals.

Carefully review the provider panel, remembering that when you sign the contract, you are agreeing to refer to physicians on the preferred panel. This list may not resemble your "normal" referral pattern. To practice quality medicine, you must feel comfortable that the physicians on the panel are of high quality, and that you can refer patients to them with confidence.

Know which diagnostic center and laboratory the plan uses. Each plan usually contracts with one or more radiology centers, and has similar contractual arrangements with other ancillary services, such as physical therapy and home nursing care. Would you be able to review radiologic studies? Are these centers of high quality?

The method of payment and other financial considerations must be clearly understood. With many managed care plans, primary care physicians receive capitation payment for caring for a panel of patients. Capitation refers to the monthly payment you receive per patient, in advance, for agreeing to provide primary care for the individual. The monthly payment will usually be constant for a given patient, but will differ for patients of various age groups, being higher for the elderly in most circumstances. For example, you have contracted with a managed care plan to care for 100 patients over the age of 65. If the monthly capitation per patient is $35, you would receive $3,500 per month directly from the plan. Some plans utilize a concept known as capitation with "withhold." Withhold refers to the agreement in advance that the primary care physician will receive the monthly capitation minus a predetermined percentage (i.e. 15%). The money withheld may be earmarked for one of several things. Some plans use it as a "specialty fund," meaning that costs incurred to pay specialists to whom the primary care physician has referred would be paid from this fund. Moneys left over at the end of the year may be "returned" to the primary care physician. Other plans may place the "withheld" money in a fund that may or may not be paid to the physician at the end of the year based upon such criteria as patient satisfaction surveys, utilization review, and quality of care parameters.

Be sure to understand how the company handles the "withhold" if this is part of the payment plan. If you stand to do better financially by referring less often and doing fewer diagnostic tests, you may find yourself thinking more about the dollars and less about what is medically correct for your patients. Try to avoid this type of contract if possible. It would be better, in my opinion, to have fixed capitation rates, not subject to reductions or withholds of any kind, so you do not allow the potential for a "bonus" to affect the care you provide your patients.

Be certain to understand that if you are paid by capitation, for what non-primary care services are you financially responsible? In other words, does the capitation payment to you include coverage for stress testing, gastrointestinal procedures, and radiologic studies? Does it include immunizations and parenteral medications administered in the office?

Patients covered under most managed care plans are responsible for a co-payment at the time of the office visit. They are aware of this, and it usually states the amount both on the patient's card and on the enrollment list you receive monthly from the managed care company. The co-payment is made to your office directly by the patient. The amount of co-payment is important in several respects. It is a source of additional income for you, above the monthly capitation. It may also serve as a disincentive for patients to come to the office unnecessarily. In other words, patients with a $20 co-payment would be less likely than those with a $5 co-payment to request an office visit for an uncomplicated upper respiratory infection. In a busy managed care practice, a higher co-pay helps to reduce office visits, and helps keep the schedule manageable. However, if the co-payment is excessively high, patients who should be calling for appointments may not do so.

Are you paid on the first of each month for the patients for whom you are responsible? If a patient enrolls in the middle of the month, and chooses you as the primary care physician, are you paid for that month? You should receive monthly from each plan a current list of those patients for whom you are being capitated, and the amount for each.

Some plans include "charge-aboves," another term unique to managed care. This refers to services you may provide to patients for which the managed care company will pay you additional money. For example, you may receive additional income from the plan for care provided to a patient during hospitalization. However, this is not the current standard. Most plans are moving away from using "charge-aboves," and instead using capitation as full payment, thereby eliminating any potential financial incentive for a physician to hospitalize a patient.

If you are negotiating with a plan which does not have capitation, but bases payment on a fee schedule, when do you receive payment? Most plans pay the physician within thirty to sixty days of receiving the bill for services. Is there a clause which allows the plan to unilaterally change the fee schedule (lower) at any time?

The method by which the plan handles requests for referrals and diagnostic procedures must be clearly understood. Most physicians are accustomed to ordering whatever tests or procedures they feel are medically indicated, and referring patients to other physicians similarly based on their medical judgment, without having to obtain approval from anyone other than the patient. With managed care, the rules have changed. Most plans require the primary care physician, as "gatekeeper" of his or her patient's health care, to obtain in advance approval from the plan to proceed with a referral or order certain diagnostic tests. Some plans use a computerized system of approval, others require someone from the physician's office to call the managed care company for such approval. If the system utilized is the latter, it may be very time-consuming, and occupy a significant amount of one of your employee's time. If you are in solo practice or in a small group, you may not be able to afford to have an employee tied up on the phone for long periods of time waiting to speak to a representative of the plan. Try to find out in advance as much about the referral process as you can, and speak with other physicians about their experiences with specific plans in this regard.

It is not safe to assume that your contract with a managed care plan will be automatically renewed each year. Ask about the renewal process before you contract with any organization. If the criteria for renewal are arbitrary, you may leave yourself vulnerable if your contract with one or more plans is not renewed. This is especially true if you are working with only a few plans, and the patients covered under these plans account for a high percentage of your income. As mentioned earlier, there is power in numbers. If you are in solo practice, or otherwise not affiliated with other physicians, you may be more susceptible to non-renewal than if you are in a group or affiliated with a large number of providers. A managed care plan is less likely to terminate or not renew a contract with a given physician if the physician is part of a group on which the plan is dependent.

Understand the steps you need to take to terminate your relationship with a plan. How much notice are you required to provide? If you resign from a plan, are you able to reapply in the future? Learn whether your status with a plan is tied to hospital privileges or is dependent upon specialty board certification.

Economic credentialing is a term with which you should be familiar. Economic data about physicians is collected and examined, and may be used to determine whether a physician is credentialed or accepted as a provider for a managed care plan. It may also affect potential renewal of a managed care contract. Factors considered include, but are not limited to, hospital admissions, length of stays, diagnostic tests, referrals, and use of other ancillary services. You should be aware prior to signing an agreement whether a managed care company utilizes such data in the credentialing or re-credentialing process.

Most physicians are accustomed to the traditional method of establishment of a patient-physician relationship. This means that one's responsibility as a physician for an individual's care does not start until you have seen the patient and accepted the responsibility. Under the guidelines of many managed care plans, however, this is quite different. The plan may stipulate that your responsibility begins as soon as a patient has "selected" you as the primary care physician. It is very important for you to be aware of this, and for your office to have an up-to-date list of patients for each plan. Be certain that your office staff and any physicians with whom you cross-cover understand this responsibility, so as not to refuse to see a patient for whom you have agreed, by contract, to provide care.

As a primary care physician, are you able to limit the number of patients for whom you are responsible under a plan? This point should be clear prior to committing yourself to a managed care organization. Are you required to be on-call 24 hours a day for the enrollees, and if so, are the physicians covering for you required to be participants in the plan in order to be compensated? Some plans place a financial obligation upon you if a patient is seen by a covering physician, in your absence, who is not a plan participant. In other words, it is possible that there is a clause in the contract which reduces payments to you if payments were made to another provider, for services rendered in your absence.

- Open vs. closed panels
- Power in numbers
- Understand the authorization procedure
- Quality of ancillary services
- Understand payment method
- Understand your responsibilities

CHAPTER 8.

THE PATIENT-PHYSICIAN RELATIONSHIP

One of the most satisfying aspects of private practice is the ability to establish close, long-lasting relationships with your patients. This is especially true for primary care medicine. You see patients and their families during periods of health and during periods of severe illness. It is not unusual for the primary care physician to be seen as a member of the family, and to be called upon for advice on non-medical matters as well.

During a busy day in the office, you will see many patients, and frequently speak to twice as many on the telephone. It is wise to remember, though, that to each patient the encounter with you is very important. When with each patient, be attentive and demonstrate concern. It is disconcerting to a patient if you appear distracted during the office visit, or if you are interrupted several times by telephone or by beeper. Instruct your office personnel not to interrupt you while with a patient, except for an emergency or unless you are expecting an important call. If you are expecting a call from a physician or the hospital, it is a good idea to let your staff know this before you go into the exam room, so they will be sure to let you know when the call occurs. Regardless, try to minimize interruptions of any kind, and if interrupted, apologize to the patient. This should be especially true when seeing a new patient, who has yet to form a strong relationship with you, and with whose history you are not yet familiar. An established patient of long-standing tends to be more understanding of interruptions.

Maintain eye contact as much as possible with your patients. Many physicians take notes while talking to patients, but try to limit this as much as possible. In my opinion, it is preferable to listen without taking notes during the history, and then to make notes, if necessary, upon leaving the exam room. Some physicians dictate each visit immediately after completion, when the findings are still fresh in their minds. For those who dictate only once or twice a day, some notations are usually needed so as not to forget important details.

Be as punctual as possible, and respect your patient's time as you would expect a patient to respect yours. Being kept waiting for a significant length of time is one of the most common sources of dissatisfaction among patients. One of the keys to staying on schedule is to start on time. Many physicians either get to the office late or start with the first patient late, and it is downhill from there. Learn to budget your time appropriately and be practical about your schedule. If you have to stop at two hospitals in the morning before getting to the office, you must take this into consideration when designing your office schedule. Double booking or over-booking appointments invariably means you will be behind schedule throughout the day. Leave room on your daily schedule for patients who need to be worked-in and for other unexpected events. If you have a day without work-ins or emergencies, it gives you a chance to catch up on paperwork, review lab work, return phone calls, or review old records.

When establishing your office schedule, several important guidelines should be followed. Decide the time you wish to begin and end the scheduled patients for the day, as well as the time allotted for lunch. Determine the amount of time you require for different types of office visits. A new patient having a complete examination (45-60 minutes) requires more time than someone coming in for follow-up for hypertension (10-15 minutes). Design your own template, and it may be necessary to try several different templates before you are satisfied that you are making the best use of your time. Time management for a physician is an integral part of your day. The more time lost in the middle of the day, the later your day will be completed. When designing a template, you must remember the role your medical assistant(s) play in the flow of the office. For example, if you have performed a complete examination and then your nurse must draw blood or perform some other procedure on the patient, you are usually able to see another patient in brief follow-up while your nurse is busy. This effective use of time can add up throughout the day, and helps to keep you on schedule as well. If despite your best efforts, you are running late, apologize to the patient when you first enter the exam room.

Being punctual is one way to demonstrate your consideration for a patient. Another is to be certain that you do everything you can to make the visit as comfortable as possible. When seeing someone for the first time, it is usually better to take the history with the patient fully clothed, and then leave the room while the patient puts on a gown. If you are male, and seeing a female patient, you should be accompanied in the room by your nurse or medical assistant during the majority of the physical exam. There should be no exception to this when performing breast, pelvic or rectal examinations. Some patients are more comfortable if there is an escort during the entire exam, and in these cases, you should respect the patient's wishes.

Fear and anxiety on the part of the patient are frequent emotions experienced during an office visit. Be aware of this. By explaining what you are doing as you go through the exam, you make the patient more comfortable and relaxed, and demonstrate your consideration. It is often helpful to inform the patient of normal findings as the exam progresses as a way to alleviate anxiety.

After completing the examination, it is important to take adequate time to explain your findings and recommendations to the patient, and allow the patient time to ask questions. If the patient has been accompanied to the office by a spouse or other family member, it is appropriate and considerate to ask if the patient wishes the individual(s) to be present during the discussion. This affords the family member the opportunity to meet you, hear what you have to say, and ask questions. Whether accompanied by a family member or not, I feel it is best to have this discussion in your consultation room, rather than in the exam room. By doing so, you demonstrate your interest in the patient, and that you are willing to take the time to discuss the visit and address any additional concerns.

Another method of showing consideration for a patient is to get back in touch with the patient as soon as possible with results of laboratory or other tests performed. Put yourself in the patient's place in this regard; most people have some degree of anxiety about the results, and the sooner you let someone know that all is well the better. Patients appreciate hearing from your office as soon as possible, and in the eyes of the patient, it is an excellent way to show your concern.

Physicians handle discussion of test results differently. Most physicians feel that it is acceptable for their nurse or medical assistant to call a patient with normal results. However, if a test result is abnormal, it is usually better for the physician to call personally. By doing so, you decrease the chance that something could be lost in translation, and importantly, provide the patient the opportunity to ask questions, as well as jointly deciding on a course of action.

Protect patient confidentiality at all times. Your office personnel should be instructed on this issue and constantly reminded of it's importance. Never discuss details about a patient within hearing distance of another. Physicians, nurses, and secretaries should be sensitive to the fact that telephone conversations may be easily overheard. When attempting to contact a patient by telephone, do not leave specific details on an answering machine, as the message may be retrieved by someone other than the patient. It is better to request that the patient return the call when able.

In establishing strong physician-patient relationships, it is of utmost importance that your patients feel that you care about them, and that they are not just a number or a chart to you. Spend a few minutes during the office visit talking about their family or job, or talking about your family, if asked. Unsolicited phone calls can go a long way towards strengthening trust and creating a bond between yourself and your patients. Calling an ill patient at the end of the day who you had seen or spoken to earlier is greatly appreciated. It also gives you the opportunity to get a progress report from the patient. Similarly, calling a patient the day after hospital discharge is a good idea. It lets the patient know that you are concerned, and gives you the chance to review the medication instructions and answer any questions, as well as to insure proper follow-up. When a patient is hospitalized, making an unsolicited call to the spouse or other family member after morning rounds is a good idea. It not only demonstrates your concern, but allows you to keep the family abreast of any new developments. By calling yourself and reaching the family, you often prevent being interrupted by a similar phone call during office hours.

When a patient is critically ill and hospitalized, the demands on your time can be substantial. Not only do you often see the patient more than once a day, and receive frequent calls from the nursing staff, but the family wants to either see you or speak to you often. It is helpful in such circumstances, to request that the family have a single representative with whom you speak each day, and who then transmits the information to the others. Meeting face-to-face with the family is a good idea, especially when there are several family members involved, when the patient's outlook is poor, or when you do not have a long-lasting, strong relationship with the patient. This type of meeting gives all concerned family members an opportunity to ask questions and gives you the opportunity to be certain that all parties have an accurate picture of the situation.

Honesty in dealing with patients is critical to the establishment of trust. Patients will respect your honesty, and this helps to establish strong relationships. Do not take advantage of patients by ordering tests which are not medically necessary, just because you have the capability of performing the tests and the patient's insurance pays for them. Intellectual dishonesty on your part can be recognized by most patients, and prevents the development of mutual trust.

You should try to keep patients' and families' expectations as realistic as possible when dealing with illness. By providing accurate, up-to-date progress reports, you help patients and families to see most situations realistically.

Avoid making guarantees about treatments or procedures. Reassuring a patient that a complication resulting from a procedure or other treatment is unlikely may be appropriate, but do not guarantee it. If you do, and a complication subsequently occurs, your promise will be remembered.

Always be an advocate for your patient. In the era of managed care, you will likely find yourself in situations when the managed care organization may not approve a referral or diagnostic test you feel is medically necessary. By going to bat for your patient, and doing everything in your power to attempt to resolve the conflict, you will go a long way in the establishment of trust.

Dealing with end-of-life issues can be very difficult for the physician. It is critical that the patient and family feel that you are there for them during this time, even when the majority of the clinical care may be provided by someone else (surgeon; oncologist). If you have been involved with a patient for a significant period of time, and the patient is in the terminal stage of illness, both the patient and family look to you for guidance and support during this time. You may no longer be intimately involved in the day-to-day clinical decision-making, but your role is just as important, if not more so. In this role, you are a friend, as well as a physician, and are perceived as such by the patient. Be certain to let the patient know that you are still there, and give him a chance to ask questions. As the physician closest to the patient, you may know best when the time has come to discontinue aggressive treatment, and emphasize symptomatic care. The patient may have previously expressed his or her wishes to you with reference to end-of-life issues. You may be the only health care provider involved in the case who is familiar with the family members, and therefore best able to effectively and honestly communicate with them.

After a patient dies, your initial expression of condolence to the family should not end your involvement with them. It is appropriate to send a card, as well as calling a week or so later to see how the family is doing. This is usually greatly appreciated, and demonstrates your concern for their well-being. In addition, this later call affords the family the opportunity to ask any question which may still be lingering in their minds. Some of the most meaningful relationships developed during practice are those which evolve after the death of a patient. Your active and supportive involvement as physician and friend in helping a patient and family deal with dying is not usually forgotten.

The difficult patient: Learning to deal with the difficult patient is also important. No physician has been fortunate to practice medicine for any period of time without having patients who are non-compliant, demanding, or otherwise a challenge to care for. The patient-physician relationship must be based on mutual trust and consideration. If a patient is dishonest with you, document it, and discuss it with him. Make it clear to the patient that you will only continue to care for him if he is honest with you, and that it will not work in any other way.

If it is apparent to you that despite discussions with the patient, you do not feel that you are able to establish or maintain such a working relationship, you may elect to terminate the relationship. If you wish to do so, you must follow established guidelines to allow the patient the opportunity to establish care elsewhere. Traditionally, this entails the delivery of a registered (return receipt requested) letter to the patient informing him that effective thirty days from the receipt of the letter you will no longer be his physician, and that until that date, you will be available for emergency care. Make it clear in the letter that a copy of the patient's medical record will be sent to the physician of the patient's choice, upon your receipt of a signed authorization from the patient. It is not necessary to discuss specific reasons in the letter for your decision to terminate the relationship. Keep a copy of the letter in the patient's chart, and inform your partners or cross-covering physicians of the effective date of termination of care. Be certain your office personnel are aware of it as well.

If you are in a group practice, it is important to discuss the ramifications of termination of a patient-physician relationship. Many groups decide that when such notification has occurred, no other member of the group will assume that individual's care. By following this rule, the original physician will not potentially be placed in a situation in the future whereby, in covering for a partner, he may be forced to care for the patient. Should such a circumstance arise, the treating physician (and patient) may feel uncomfortable, and the malpractice risk intensified.

Non-compliance is a major problem for most physicians. It is important to address this issue with your patients on a regular basis. If you suspect non-compliance, be certain that misinformation or miscommunication is not responsible. A patient may have misunderstood your instructions. For example, with reference to anti-hypertensive medication, a patient may have believed that you meant for him to take only the original prescription, and to stop it once that was completed. Review your instructions and write them down for the patient.

If it is apparent to you that miscommunication or misunderstanding is not at the root of the compliance issue, but that the patient has no intention of following your instructions, document this clearly in the record. Make it clear to the patient that he or she must take responsibility for their health and their actions.

A key to a strong patient-physician relationship is the active participation of the patient in all aspects of his or her care. When discussing treatment options or preventive health measures, it is appropriate for the physician to make recommendations, but to, at all times, involve the patient in the decision-making process. A patient may ask you to assist in making a difficult decision, and you may feel comfortable in doing so. However, the ultimate decision is always the patient's to make. Make it clear to your patient that if your recommendation is not followed, you will not abandon them, and you will continue to be their physician.

An example of this would be if a patient with chest pain, for whom you have recommended hospitalization, decides instead to go home. It is appropriate for you to then attempt to maximize the patient's care, and maintain as close contact with the patient as possible. By doing so, the patient is not abandoned, knows you are still available should the need arise, and will be more likely to contact you for continued problems.

It is appropriate for a primary care physician to discuss end-of-life issues with his patients, preferably when the patient is well. Such discussions are easier if the patient-physician relationship is strong, and the discussions themselves may further strengthen the bond. By bringing up the topics of living wills and advance directives, the physician demonstrates concern for his patient and by beginning such discussions during a period of well-being, allows ample time for thoughtful consideration of various options. This is an area where patients will often rely on the physician for advice and guidance, and yet the physician should make it clear that no matter what the patient's preferences are, he will support the decision(s). By initiating the dialogue early, as well as learning and documenting the patient's wishes, both the physician and patient are better able to deal with critical decisions during difficult times. Many physicians are uncomfortable discussing living wills and other advance directives with patients. However, I encourage all primary care physicians to not only be knowledgeable in these areas, but to assume an active role with their patients in this regard.

- Every patient encounter is important
- Punctuality
- Communicate openly and in terms patient can understand
- Leave time for questions
- Confidentiality
- HONESTY; TRUST; CONCERN; CONSIDERATION
- End-of-life issues
- Involve patient in all aspects of decision-making

CHAPTER 9.   TELEPHONE MEDICINE

Very little, if any, training in telephone medicine occurs during residency. Some residents, during rotations with community preceptors, are exposed to this portion of private practice, however, formal training is usually lacking or insufficient. Mastering the skills utilized in telephone medicine takes significant time and experience, but the recommendations forthcoming should serve as a valuable starting point for physicians starting out in private practice.

Always protect patient confidentiality when speaking on the telephone. If you are not certain that you are speaking with the patient directly, do not reveal confidential information. A patient may not wish test results to be discussed with anyone else, including a spouse. In fact, the patient may not want anyone else to know that he or she even visited the office. It is helpful to ask the patient at the completion of the office visit how best to reach him to discuss the results of any pending tests. If you reach an answering machine when you call the patient, it is best to request that the patient return the call to discuss results, rather than be specific when leaving the message.

It is not uncommon for an insurance company, attorney's office, or managed care company to call a physician's office requesting information about a patient. Never discuss or release information over the telephone about a patient without the patient's permission. Be certain that your office personnel are familiar with this policy. It is appropriate to respond to such requests by informing the caller that your office requires a properly executed release of information from the patient before you will discuss anything.

As mentioned earlier, when dealing with results of laboratory studies or other diagnostic tests, you should have in place in your office a system to manage phone calls from patients to discuss results. Many physicians allow their nurses or medical assistants to inform patients of normal results, and to document the conversation in the medical record. For abnormal results, it is usually best for the physician to contact the patient personally. In certain clinical situations, it may be advisable to ask the patient to come to the office to discuss or review the results.

In a primary care practice, many telephone calls are received on a daily basis from patients with problems, ranging from side effects of medications to a new symptom complex. Many patients request or expect to speak directly to the physician in each instance. In a busy practice, it is unrealistic to believe that the physician would have the time to speak personally to each and every patient who called. It is helpful to explain to your patients your office policy for handling phone calls, and the reasoning behind it. It should be clear to your patients that your nurse or medical assistant will discuss the situation with you, and that you, as the physician, will decide on a course of action. Many patients are under the impression that because they discussed their cases with the nurse, that the nurse is the one making the clinical decision. In this view, it is important that at the end of the telephone call, your nurse or medical assistant clearly says: "I will discuss this with the doctor, and I will call you back."

There will be times that a patient does not want to discuss a symptom or complaint with the nurse, or feels uncomfortable doing so. If this is stated by the patient, it should be respected, and it is appropriate for the nurse to inform the patient that you will return the call when time allows. If it is your policy to return nonurgent calls at the end of the day, your nurse should let the patient know this.

One of the most important aspects of telephone medicine is to recognize symptoms of an urgent or emergent nature. It is not usually difficult for a physician to do so, but your office personnel may not have sufficient training or experience in this area. It is not safe to assume that, even if you have employees with medical experience, they are capably trained to perform this task. You should spend meaningful time with your personnel in training in this regard. They should learn to quickly recognize symptoms which should immediately be brought to your attention. It is critical that your employees understand that it is always better to check with you if there is any question at all of a possible urgent problem, rather than to risk putting the patient off, and thus delaying care. By working closely with your personnel, you may also avoid a situation when a patient is instructed to come directly to your office, when the appropriate thing to do instead is to call the paramedics or an ambulance. If a situation arises when you feel one of your employees did not handle a telephone call appropriately, use it as an educational tool, and be constructive rather than critical in your subsequent discussion.

Instruct your employees under what circumstances you should be interrupted about a clinical situation. If you are in the middle of a complete examination with a patient, and another patient calls with chest pain, it is usually best to inform you of the call as soon as possible, so you will be able to direct the patient as to a course of action. The same approach may be appropriate in many other clinical scenarios. On the other hand, your staff should know which problems can wait until you have finished with the patient you are with, and which problems can wait until the end of the morning (or the day).

Your staff should routinely obtain the patient's chart before approaching you with a question. Even if you are very familiar with the patient, record documentation is necessary after deciding what to do. In addition, if you are part of a group practice, there may be an entry in the record of which you were not aware, and which may affect your decision.

Develop a system which allows you to be aware of patient calls in a timely way, but which also is not overly disruptive of your office schedule. Each physician will establish a system of his own; your office personnel should work under it's guidelines, yet feel comfortable to approach you with an emergency at any time. A popular system is to set aside time every one to two hours to review telephone calls which had been received. In so doing, you may ask several patients to come in to be seen, and call in medication for others. Your patients appreciate a return call within a reasonable period of time, so as not to be disruptive of their own day. If it is your practice to keep available appointment slots open for same-day work-ins, regular review of phone calls allows you to fill these slots with appropriate visits.

Some physicians reserve time only at the end of the morning and the end of the day to review calls with the nurse. This may be less disruptive of the schedule, but risks delaying treatment of symptomatic patients, and may lead to dissatisfied patients as well (especially if the patient has been waiting hours for a return phone call). In addition, by holding numerous charts until the end of the day, the physician and his nurse often work longer hours than would otherwise be necessary. My recommendation is to review and discuss non-emergent problems on a regular basis throughout the day (perhaps every one to two hours), and if a personal call from you to the patient is required, to try to do this at the end of the morning session or at the end of the day.

Good telephone medicine and proper medical record documentation are intimately related. You should document each telephone conversation in the patient's chart. This is true whether the patient or your office initiated the call. If the call was made by the patient, it is important to document the reason for the call, and your recommendation(s). If you suggest or recommend an office visit or emergency room visit, and the patient declines, this should be clearly stated in the chart. Any medication called in to a pharmacy should be written in the medical record, as well as your discussion about possible adverse effects. If the call was an unsolicited one made by you, also notate this in the record, as it documents your follow-up of a problem and your concern for the patient.

- Confidentiality
- Training of office personnel
- Documentation in the medical record

CHAPTER 10.   CODING

In the practice of medicine, coding refers to two separate but equally important areas. One is the code(s) which applies to the diagnosis (or diagnoses) for which the patient was seen on the date of the visit. The second is the "CPT" code, which stands for "Current Procedural Terminology," and is the code which identifies the level of service provided.

The diagnostic codes are extensive, but relatively easy to use. Comprehensive lists of diagnoses and diagnostic procedures are available and easily accessible to physicians. There are several important factors of which you must be aware in the use of diagnostic codes. One is clinical applicability. This refers to the fact that the diagnostic code you assign to a visit must clinically apply to THAT visit. In other words, if you are following a patient with diabetes, but you have just seen the patient because of an upper respiratory infection, you should use the diagnostic code for URI. Applicability pertains to procedures as well as to visits. If you are billing for the interpretation of an electrocardiogram, the diagnostic code used must apply to the procedure. For example, URI would not be an appropriate code in this circumstance, and, if used, would result in non-payment. The payors, such as Medicare, can provide you with acceptable diagnostic codes for any billable procedure.

Another area of importance is accountability. This refers to the fact that you, as the physician, are ultimately responsible and accountable for the diagnostic code(s) utilized. If an incorrect code was used by one of your employees, and this results in improper payment to you, you are the one held responsible.

The correct use of diagnostic coding has significant financial implications as well. If more than one physician is involved in the care of a hospitalized patient, payment to the physicians by a third-party payor (such as Medicare) is usually dependent upon the use of proper (and different) codes. For example, if you, as the primary care physician, and a cardiologist are both following a patient in the coronary care unit, and you both use the same diagnostic code for billing purposes, one of you may not be paid. In this case, the insurance carrier may interpret the billing as duplicate services, and deny payment for one of the physicians. On the other hand, if you utilize an alternative, yet still appropriate, diagnosis, it is likely you will both receive payment. For the case outlined above, if the patient is diabetic, and as part of the care, you are monitoring and treating the diabetes, it would be better to use Diabetes as the diagnostic code for your services.

Physicians must also be aware that hospitals are dependent on thorough and correct coding in order to receive payment for inpatient care. In most hospitals, the medical records department has an individual or individuals who are responsible for proper diagnostic coding of the chart after patients have been discharged. You may be asked to complete a face-sheet listing the medical diagnosis(es) pertinent to the patient's admission, as well as any diagnostic procedures performed during the hospitalization. In other institutions, the records department may complete the face-sheet and, prior to submitting the bill to the payor, will ask you to review the diagnosis(es) for accuracy.

Learning and understanding the coding system for the physician's professional component of service provided is not an easy task. Every practicing physician must be comfortable and knowledgeable with this system, as it is now utilized by virtually every third-party payor. This coding system is the method by which the physician communicates to the payor what level of professional service was provided for the patient, and, therefore, what reimbursement may be due to the physician. The codes are commonly referred to as "evaluation and management codes."

Presently, there are codes for outpatient care, hospital care, and long-term facility care. There are different codes for some sections for established patients and for new patients. There are important documentation requirements if you are working with a medical student, resident, or fellow, and you are billing for the services provided. It is extremely important that each physician understand the meaning of each code, utilize the proper code, and be certain that the written note in the medical record contain all necessary documentation.

For the purpose of this discussion, a new patient is defined as one who has not received professional services from the physician or another physician of the same specialty belonging to the same group, within the previous three years. In other words, if you are covering for a partner, and seeing one of his or her active patients, even though the patient is new to you, for billing purposes the patient is considered an established patient.

Medicare and other third-party payors may periodically audit the medical records of a physician in order to see if the physician's progress notes have proper documentation to support the billings. Physicians may be at risk should the payor determine that insufficient documentation exists in the records to substantiate the submitted bills. When an audit is performed, typically a relatively small number of charts are reviewed. The payor uses only what is present in the record with which to make a determination, so complete and proper documentation is crucial. I will outline several examples of outpatient coding below, but I encourage each resident to obtain a coding booklet with which to become familiar and to use as a handy reference. An excellent reference guide may be obtained from:

Healthcare Quality Consultants
20 New Hampshire Drive, Suite D-7
New Britain, CT 06052

It is entitled: CODING AND DOCUMENTATION QUICK REFERENCE BOOKLET, Physician's Professional Component.

For a new patient being seen in the office, there are five codes which can be used. These are: 99201 (problem focused), 99202 (expanded problem focused), 99203 (detailed), 99204 (comprehensive), and 99205 (comprehensive). Although both 99204 and 99205 are considered comprehensive, the difference lies in the complexity of the medical decision-making. The requirements for 99205 include medical decision-making of high complexity, whereas the requirements for 99204 include decision-making of moderate complexity. This level of complexity must be clearly documented in the progress note. Both codes require documentation of chief complaint, extended history of present illness, complete past history, family history, social history, and complete review of systems, as well as EITHER complete multi-system examination OR complete single system specialty examination. Codes 99201, 99202, and 99203 are for lower intensity of service, but each has it's own documentation requirements.

Analogous codes exist for established patients seen in the outpatient setting. These are 99211, 99212, 99213, 99214, and 99215. 99211 is a unique code in that when using this code, the physician does not have to be present or actually see the patient. An example of this would be when a patient comes to the office for a blood pressure check, has it performed by the nurse, who then writes the note in the chart, and the note is cosigned by the physician. All of the other codes in this category require the presence of the physician.

Outpatient consultations for either new OR established patients have codes which range from 99241 (problem-focused) to 99245 (comprehensive). It is important that the physician requesting the consultation document the request in the medical record, and that the consulting physician label the note as a consultative one.

Inpatient hospital visit codes are the same for new and established patients. Initial hospital visit codes are used for the initial encounter with the patient by the admitting physician with reference to a specific hospitalization. The codes for these encounters are 99221, 99222, and 99223, corresponding to detailed, comprehensive with moderate medical decision-making complexity, and comprehensive with high medical decision-making complexity. Occasionally, a physician will admit a patient over the telephone, and subsequently see the patient the following morning. In this instance, use the date you actually see the patient as the initial hospital day, not the actual date of admission. Follow-up inpatient visit codes are 99231, 99232, and 99233, which correspond to problem-focused, expanded problem-focused, and detailed visits. There are specific documentation requirements for each of these codes, which must be met in order to justify payment. A progress note in the hospital chart must be written for each corresponding billed visit. Codes 99238 and 99239 are used for hospital discharge services, which include instruction to the patient and family, completion of prescriptions and other forms, and preparation of the discharge summary for the medical record. Use code 99238 if the TOTAL time spent in this process was thirty minutes or less, and code 99239 if the time spent was greater than thirty minutes. Be certain to document in the medical record the total time spent in the discharge process.

Initial inpatient consultation codes are 99251 (problem-focused), 99252 (expanded problem-focused), 99253 (detailed), 99254 (comprehensive with moderate medical decision-making complexity), and 99255 (comprehensive with high medical decision-making complexity). The same guidelines pertain to inpatient consultations as to outpatient consultations with reference to the need for documentation by the referring physician of the request for the consultation, and documentation by the consultant that the visit is a consultation.

Follow-up or subsequent inpatient consultation codes are 99261 (problem-focused), 99262 (expanded problem-focused), and 99263 (detailed). These codes should be used either to complete the initial consultation or when subsequent consultative visits are requested by the referring physician. An example of the latter would be if the primary care physician requests a surgical consultation, which is performed on day 1 of a hospital stay, and, five days later, the primary care physician requests the surgeon to see the patient again.

If a consultant feels that, after performing the initial consultation, it is medically necessary to see the patient daily in follow-up along with the primary care physician, follow-up consultation codes should be used only for one or two days after the initial consultation. For visits subsequent to that, the consultant should utilize follow-up inpatient hospital visit codes (99231, 99232 or 99233). For billing purposes, it is important that when more than one physician is using follow-up hospital visit codes for a given patient for the same days, that different (and appropriate) diagnostic codes be used by each physician. For example, a primary care physician consults a gastroenterologist with reference to a patient admitted with pancreatitis. If the consultant follows the patient for more than two or three days, and the primary care physician and consultant both subsequently bill the insurance company (for the follow-up visits) using the diagnostic code for pancreatitis, it is likely that only one of the physicians will be paid. However, if the patient also was diabetic, and the primary care physician was managing this aspect of the patient's care, it would be better for billing purposes for the primary care physician to use the code for diabetes when billing for the follow-up visits.

Codes for critical care should be used when caring for an unstable critically ill or critically injured patient. The medical conditions which usually require critical care include shock, respiratory failure, sepsis, circulatory failure, and central nervous system failure. Utilize code 99291 when billing for the first hour of critical care services, and code 99292 for each additional thirty minutes in a given 24-hour period. Again, document the total time spent in the medical record.

I have referred earlier to the terms moderately complex medical decision-making and high complexity medical decision-making, and I will try to clarify these further. For the purposes of appropriate billing, medical decision-making refers to the complexity of deciding about a treatment option and/or the complexity of diagnosis. For decision-making of moderate complexity, the number of diagnoses or treatment options should be multiple, and the risk of complications moderate. An example of this would be a new, acute illness such as pneumonia with accompanying systemic symptoms. Decision-making of high complexity usually involves a high risk of complications and an extensive number of diagnoses or treatment options. An example would be an acute illness which carries a threat of life, such as acute myocardial infarction.

Modifiers are codes, usually two-digit ones, which may be used to modify an evaluation and management code. The two-digit number is added after the full five-digit one. An example would be 99205-25, in which case the modifier is 25. A modifier should be used when the physician wishes to include circumstances which change the service provided. One of the most frequently used modifiers is 25, which should be used when a PROCEDURE and a VISIT are both performed (and billed) at the same visit. By adding this modifier, the physician is communicating to the payor that a procedure (which was not a scheduled or routine one) was performed in addition to the evaluation and management visit. An example of this would be a patient who comes to the office with abdominal pain and rectal bleeding, and that in addition to history and physical examination, the physician feels that sigmoidoscopy is indicated, and proceeds with the performance of same. In this case, the modifier would follow the office visit code (i.e. 99203-25), followed by the code for sigmoidoscopy.

All physicians should understand the importance of accurate and honest coding when submitting bills to patients and to third-party payors, and that appropriate documentation in the record is mandatory for each patient encounter. Documentation must be done on the day of the visit, and cannot be done at a future date when a physician learns of an impending audit. It is unwise and a huge financial risk to bill payors without complete and thorough documentation. Understanding and learning this before beginning practice will pay off in the long run.

- Understand diagnostic coding and applicability of same
- Understand CPT codes
- Medical record documentation

REFERENCES

1. Connally N. T. "Nurturing the Physician-Patient Relationship." Today's Internist, May/June 1997:12-17.

2. Reney C, Lagasse E. L. Coding and Documentation Quick Reference Booklet, 1996.

3. Fox Y. "Joining an Established Practice." Today's Internist, March/April 1997: 41-42.

4. Grimaldi P. A Glossary of Managed Care Terms. Nurs Manage Sp Supp, October 1996: 4, 7, 8.

5. Ethics Manual. Third Edition. American College of Physicians, 1993.

6. Cherkin DC, Grothaus L, Wagner EH. "The Effect of Office Visit Copayments on Utilization in a Health Maintenance Organization." Med Care, 1989; 27 (11): 1036-1045.

7. Shapiro MF, Ware JE, Sherbourne CD. "Effects of Cost Sharing on Seeking Care for Serious and Minor Symptoms." Ann of Int Med, 1986; 104: 246-251.

8. Nash D, Future Practice Alternatives in Medicine, Second Edition. New York, Igaku-Shoin Medical Publishers, 1993.

RAPID LEARNING AND RETENTION THROUGH THE MEDMASTER SERIES:

CLINICAL NEUROANATOMY MADE RIDICULOUSLY SIMPLE, by S. Goldberg
CLINICAL BIOCHEMISTRY MADE RIDICULOUSLY SIMPLE, by S. Goldberg
CLINICAL ANATOMY MADE RIDICULOUSLY SIMPLE, by S. Goldberg
CLINICAL PHYSIOLOGY MADE RIDICULOUSLY SIMPLE, by S. Goldberg
CLINICAL MICROBIOLOGY MADE RIDICULOUSLY SIMPLE, by M. Gladwin and B. Trattler
CLINICAL PHARMACOLOGY MADE RIDICULOUSLY SIMPLE, by J.M. Olson
OPHTHALMOLOGY MADE RIDICULOUSLY SIMPLE, by S. Goldberg
PSYCHIATRY MADE RIDICULOUSLY SIMPLE, by W.V. Good and J. Nelson
CLINICAL PSYCHOPHARMACOLOGY MADE RIDICULOUSLY SIMPLE, by J. Preston and J. Johnson
ACUTE RENAL INSUFFICIENCY MADE RIDICULOUSLY SIMPLE, by C. Rotellar
MEDICAL BOARDS STEP 1 MADE RIDICULOUSLY SIMPLE, by A. Carl
MEDICAL BOARDS STEP 2 MADE RIDICULOUSLY SIMPLE, by A. Carl
MEDICAL BOARDS STEP 3 MADE RIDICULOUSLY SIMPLE, by A. Carl
BEHAVIORAL MEDICINE MADE RIDICULOUSLY SIMPLE, by F. Seitz and J. Carr
USMLE BEHAVIORAL SCIENCE MADE RIDICULOUSLY SIMPLE, by F.S. Sierles
ACID-BASE, FLUIDS, AND ELECTROLYTES MADE RIDICULOUSLY SIMPLE, by R. Preston
THE FOUR-MINUTE NEUROLOGIC EXAM, by S. Goldberg
MEDICAL SPANGLISH, by T. Espinoza-Abrams
THE DIFFICULT PATIENT, by E. Sohr
CLINICAL ANATOMY AND PATHOPHYSIOLOGY FOR THE HEALTH PROFESSIONAL, by J.V. Stewart
CONSCIOUSNESS, INFORMATION, AND MEANING: THE ORIGIN OF THE MIND, by S. Goldberg
PREPARING FOR MEDICAL PRACTICE MADE RIDICULOUSLY SIMPLE, by D.M. Lichtstein
NEUROLOGIC LOCALIZATION (MacIntosh computer program), by S. Goldberg

Try your bookstore for these. For further information and ordering send for the MedMaster catalog at MedMaster, P.O. Box 640028, Miami FL 33164.